BEST of the BEST from
Bell's Best
COOKBOOK

BEST of the BEST from
Bell's Best
COOKBOOK

The Most Popular Recipes
from the Four Classic Bell's Best
Cookbooks

COMPILED BY
TelecomPioneers of Mississippi

PUBLISHED BY
QUAIL RIDGE PRESS
Preserving America's Food Heritage

Library of Congress Cataloging-in-Publication Data

Best of the best from Bell's best cookbook : the most popular recipes from the four classic Bell's best cookbooks / Telephone Pioneers of America, Mississippi Chapter No. 36.
   p. cm. –
Includes index.
ISBN-13: 978-1-893062-93-1
ISBN-10: 1-893062-93-7
   1. Cookery, American. I. Telephone Pioneers of America. Mississippi Chapter no. 36
   TX715.B485612 2006
   641.5--dc22   2006018344

ISBN-13: 978-1-893062-93-1 • ISBN-10: 1-893062-93-7

First Edition
Printed in Canada

Design by Cyndi Clark.
Cover photo by Greg Campbell.
On the cover: Friendship Tea (page 14), Marinated Greek Salad (page 86), Popeye's Biscuits (page 41), Buttermilk Fried Chicken (page 152), Chocolate Chip Cheesecake (page 211), and Party Cookies (page 218).

QUAIL RIDGE PRESS
P. O. Box 123 • Brandon, MS 39043 • 1-800-343-1583
email: info@quailridge.com • www.quailridge.com

Contents

Our Mission

To provide rewarding community service experiences and fellowship opportunities for all of our employees, retirees, and their families.

To provide value to sponsoring companies by generating brand visibility, building teamwork, developing leadership skills of employees, and demonstrating the corporate social commitment.

To enable our Life Members to maintain strong ties to our sponsoring companies.

To be well-known as volunteers meeting a variety of community needs, with special emphasis on education.

BELLSOUTH VOLUNTEERS

@Work in Communities

Preface

The *Bell's Best* cookbooks have been a very profitable venture for the Mississippi Pioneers since the first edition was published in 1981. The sales provide funding for many projects that improve the communities in which we live. While the original *Bell's Best 1* continues to be the most popular and best selling, the other books have found their way into many households.

Many customers have praised the recipes found in all four *Bell's Best* cookbooks. Countless people have enjoyed the meals prepared using these four cookbooks. The requests for a book that combines the "Best of the Best" has been a constant refrain from many of these cooks. This book is the result of those requests.

Pioneers across the state submitted their selections of time-tested and proven recipes from all four books. These selections were compiled, sorted, and now grace the pages of this cookbook as a collection of the best recipes of the BELL'S BEST COOKBOOK SERIES.

This compilation is possible due to the countless hours of work by many Pioneers over the past twenty-five years. I would like to thank every one of them for their dedication and tireless efforts. Numerous projects benefiting education and community organizations have been funded by the proceeds of these books. There are no words to fully convey the appreciation due to the active and retired employees who have made this possible.

An immeasurable debt of gratitude is owed to a very special volunteer who has been at the heart of our organization for a long time. Many projects, including the publishing of this book, have largely depended on her dedication to the success of the MS Pioneers. She has made a difference in the lives of many people and continues to be a driving force in all of our endeavors. Pioneer Partner Margie Sasser has given so much to so many. It is only fitting that we dedicate this book to her as a small token of our appreciation.

This collection from *Bell's Best 1, 2, 3,* and *4,* I hope, will be the next essential cookbook for every household. It has been a joy to work on this project with the "Best of the Best"—the MS Pioneers.

Billy Harbour
Project Chairman

Note from the Publisher

Quail Ridge Press was honored to be able to participate in the development and publication of the *Best of the Best from Bell's Best Cookbook*. We have long been familiar with the BELL'S BEST COOKBOOK SERIES, as each has contributed a wonderful sampling of their recipes to the Mississippi edition of our BEST OF THE BEST STATE COOKBOOK SERIES.

The down-home, family-favorites in the BELL'S BEST COOKBOOK SERIES are exactly the kind of recipes we seek to preserve in our BEST OF THE BEST STATE COOKBOOK SERIES—recipes that have been developed and perfected over generations; recipes that are legendary within a family and are now being shared with other families.

Each cookbook in the BELL'S BEST COOKBOOK SERIES has been reprinted many times. The total sales of all four titles exceed well over 700,000 copies. The cookbooks continue to be popular with young cooks as well as longtime cooks.

The TelecomPioneers of Mississippi, the organization of employees, retirees, and families of the telecommunications industry in Mississippi, are the force that have made the *Bell's Best* cookbooks the success they are. The Pioneers are all volunteers who have given their time and energy to a variety of projects and activities that enrich our community.

I speak for all of us at Quail Ridge Press in saying that we are proud to be a part of this new cookbook that offers the finest recipes from the BELL'S BEST COOKBOOK SERIES. This new cookbook will continue to provide the Pioneers with the revenue that finances their worthy projects and will enable Quail Ridge Press to continue our goal of Preserving America's Food Heritage.

Gwen McKee, President
Quail Ridge Press
Brandon, Mississippi

Contributing Cookbooks

Bell's Best 1

Since the inception of Pioneering, the priority has been "Answering the Call of Those in Need," whether natural disaster, education of our children, care of the elderly, or the varied needs of Mississippi communities. Realizing that fulfilling this mission would take lots and lots of dollars, Pioneer leaders started to look for a way to raise the needed funds. Although not without apprehension, it was decided that a cookbook filled with recipes from our own employees may be a way to raise the money. After much planning and hard work by Pioneer volunteers, in October of 1981, *Bell's Best,* containing over 700 pages of recipes, was completed and the first order of 10,000 books was placed. Its success, while not anticipated, was very much embraced by Pioneers. Today, twenty-five years and 459,000 copies later, *Bell's Best* has become a household word in kitchens all over the United States. It is shipped weekly from the Pioneer office in Jackson, Mississippi, to customers throughout the United States and overseas.

Bell's Best 2

So many recipes were collected for *Bell's Best* that it proved impossible to include all of them in one book, so in 1982, *Bell's Best 2* was created. It includes all recipes collected but not included in *Bell's Best,* plus more collected from employees and retirees. It contains 660 pages of recipes from Mississippi cooks.

Bell's Best 3: Savory Classics

Always looking for ways to generate funds for our growing list of projects and programs, in 1992 the Pioneers decided it was time for a new *Bell's Best*. This colorful book contains 754 pages of recipes, including a large party food section, a lite cooking section, and as always, lots of favorite recipes from our employees and retirees.

Bell's Best 4: The Next Generation

Our active employees, not having lots of time to spend in the kitchen, wanted a "quick and easy" book. In 2001, they contributed their favorite quick and easy recipes, along with recipes shared by our retirees, and *Bell's Best 4* was published.

It should be noted that all of our Bell's Best books can be purchased from our website at www.bellsouthmspioneers.org, or by calling our Pioneer office in Jackson at (601) 961-1993, or by using the order form on page 286.

Beverages and Appetizers

1876
Bell's Centennial Model

"My word! It talks!" exclaimed Emperor Dom Pedro of Brazil when this early phone was demonstrated by Alexander Graham Bell at the Centennial Exposition in Philadelphia on June 25, 1876. One of the judges called the invention "the most wonderful thing in America." Bell's success with the telephone came as a direct result of his attempts to improve the telegraph.

Just three months prior, while working with fellow inventor Thomas Watson, Bell shouted, "Mr. Watson, come here. I want you!" after spilling battery acid on a transimter. Watson, working in the next room, heard Bell's voice through the wire. Watson had received the first telephone call, and quickly went to answer it.

River Commission Punch

18 fresh lemons
18 fresh oranges
1 cup water
3 cups sugar

1 (48-ounce) can sweetened
  pineapple juice
5 quarts ginger ale

Squeeze juice from lemons and oranges, saving rind from 2 lemons and 2 oranges. Cut up and cook rinds in water and sugar for 3–4 minutes. Discard rinds and strain juice into large container. Add lemon, orange, and pineapple juices, and ginger ale. If necessary, add enough water to make 5 quarts. Mix well. Freeze in quart containers. Thaw frozen mixture for 1–3 hours.

Margie Sasser, Edwards, MS (Book 3)

Pink Bride Punch

1 (3-ounce) package strawberry
  gelatin
1 cup boiling water
1 package strawberry Kool-Aid
2 quarts cold water

2½ cups sugar
1 (48-ounce) pineapple juice
1 (10-ounce) bottle 7-Up
2 pints pineapple sherbet

Dissolve gelatin in boiling water. Dissolve Kool-Aid in cold water. Combine mixtures. Add sugar; mix well; then add pineapple juice and 7-Up. Add sherbet when ready to serve.

Dot Sykes, Jackson South Council (Book 1)

Bourbon Punch

1 fifth bourbon
3 quarts ginger ale

½ pint grenadine
1 pint ReaLemon juice

Mix all ingredients and serve.

Yvonne Roberson, Natchez Council (Book 1)

Coffee Punch

1 gallon coffee, slightly
  sweetened

2–3 quarts milk
1 gallon vanilla ice cream

Make coffee by regular directions and let cool. Add milk and chopped ice cream. Serves 50–60.

Doris P. Kelly, Jackson North Council (Book 2)

Lime Slush Punch

½ cup sugar
1 (3-ounce) package lime-
  flavored gelatin
2 cups boiling water
⅓ cup lemon juice

3 cups unsweetened pineapple
  juice
1 cup cold water
1 (64-ounce) bottle ginger ale,
  chilled

Dissolve sugar and gelatin in boiling water in a large bowl; stir in juices and cold water. Cover and freeze overnight. Remove from freezer 1 hour before serving. Place in a punch bowl and break into chunks. Add ginger ale. Stir until slushy. Yields 1 gallon.

Angela L. McCoy, Jackson Council (Book 3)

Friendship Tea

1 (18-ounce) jar Tang
1 cup sugar
½ cup presweetened
  lemonade mix
½ cup instant tea

1 (3-ounce) package apricot-
  flavored gelatin
2½ teaspoons ground cinnamon
1 teaspoon ground cloves
Boiling water

Combine first 7 ingredients in large bowl, stirring well. Store mix in an airtight container. To serve, place 1½ tablespoons mix in each cup. Add 1 cup boiling water and stir. So good!

Pat Day, Natchez, MS (Book 4)

Pauline's Eggnog

This is my mom's recipe—a favorite every holiday season!

2 pints whipping cream
3 eggs
Bourbon

Sugar, to taste
Milk

You will need 3 mixing bowls. In the first bowl, beat whipping cream until stiff peaks form. Separate eggs and put whites in the second mixing bowl; beat until stiff. In the third bowl, beat egg yolks with 1 jigger of bourbon per egg until creamy. Blend the 3 mixtures together in a punch bowl and add the sugar to taste and milk for thinning. Your mixture will be very thick. Serves 6–8.

Note: You may want to increase amounts depending on number in your party.

Paulette Fancher, Greenwood, MS (Book 4)

Wassail

1 gallon apple cider
6 long cinnamon sticks
48 whole cloves
3 teaspoons whole allspice

1½–2 cups sugar
1 cup orange juice
6 tablespoons lemon juice

In a large saucepan over medium heat, bring all ingredients to boil. Simmer 10 minutes, stirring occasionally. Strain and pour into punch bowl or crockpot. Serve warm. Makes 20 servings.

Kathy Estes, Tupelo Council (Book 3)

Italian Mocha

1 cup instant coffee
1 cup granulated sugar

½ cup cocoa
4½ cups dry milk

Mix in blender until powdered. Store in airtight container. Use 2 tablespoons mix to 8 ounces of hot water.

Joyce Trapp (Book 3)

Indonesian Chocolate

½ cup Hershey's cocoa
½ cup sugar
¼ teaspoon cinnamon
1 cup water

3 cups milk
Whipped cream
Cinnamon sticks, for garnish

Combine cocoa, sugar, and cinnamon in saucepan. Add water slowly, stirring until smooth. Place over low heat; bring to a boil for 2 minutes, stirring constantly. Stir in milk; heat thoroughly, but do not boil. Serve hot with a spoonful of whipped cream and a cinnamon stick in each cup. Yields 6 generous servings.

Brenda Beck, Tupelo Council (Book 1)

Bacon and Tomato Cups

8 slices bacon
1 medium tomato
½ small onion, or 1 bunch
   green onions
⅔ cup grated Swiss cheese

½ cup mayonnaise
1 teaspoon basil
1 (10-ounce) can Hungry
   Jack biscuits

Preheat oven to 375º. Finely chop bacon, tomato, and onion. Mix all ingredients except biscuits. Spray mini muffin pans with Pam. Peel off layers of biscuits. There are 3 layers in each biscuit. Line each muffin cup with one biscuit layer and press into pan. Put a spoonful of mixture into each biscuit-filled tin. Bake about 15 minutes or until brown enough to suit you. One recipe will make 30 biscuit cups.

Fredonia Granholm, Grenada, MS (Book 4)

Tomato Sandwich Bites

1 pound bacon, fried and
   crumbled
½ cup mayonnaise

1 teaspoon Dijon mustard
Bread slices
Roma tomatoes, sliced thin

Mix first 3 ingredients. Cut bread slices with cookie cutter. Spread mixture over cut bread and top with Roma tomatoes.

Renee Willoughby, Jackson, MS (Book 4)

Bacon-Wrapped Shrimp Appetizers

CHILI DIP:

¾ cup mayonnaise
3 tablespoons chopped sweet pickles
1 tablespoon chopped pimento-stuffed olives

1½ teaspoons grated onion
1 tablespoon chili powder
1 hard-boiled egg, chopped

Mix all ingredients and chill.

SHRIMP:

⅓ cup butter or margarine, melted
1½ teaspoons chili powder
1 clove garlic, minced

16 shrimp, cooked, peeled and deveined
8 slices bacon

Mix butter, chili powder and garlic together; dip shrimp. Slice bacon in half and wrap each shrimp; fasten with toothpicks or skewers. Place on rack in broiler pan and broil 3 inches from source of heat, about 5 minutes. Serve with chilled Chili Dip.

Jeanette Boyd, Gulf Coast Council (Book 1)

Crabmeat Sandwiches

1 (8-ounce) package cream cheese, softened
1 (7.5-ounce) can crabmeat, drained
2 tablespoons mayonnaise

2 tablespoons chili sauce
1 onion, chopped
1 (4-ounce) can shrimp, drained
Dash of Worcestershire

Put all in mixer; mix well. Spread on bread, then cut into finger sandwiches and serve.

Dot Miller, Meridian Council (Book 1)

Hot Crab Pickups

1 (7-ounce) can crabmeat, drained
1 stick margarine, softened
1 (7-ounce) jar Old English sharp cheese spread
2 tablespoons mayonnaise
½ teaspoon McCormick seasoned salt
½ teaspoon garlic salt
1 (6-count) package English muffins

Mix all ingredients and spread mixture on English muffins. Cut in quarters and freeze on cookie sheet. When frozen, place in plastic bags. When ready to serve, take out what you need, place on cookie sheet, and put under broiler until bubbly.

J. C. Rainey, Sr., Hattiesburg Council (Book 3)

Buffalo Wings

12 chicken wings
2 tablespoons Tabasco
1½ tablespoons red wine vinegar
2 tablespoons butter
Celery sticks
Blue cheese salad dressing

Cut wing tips off at joints; discard. Cut each wing in half at joint. On broiler pan rack, arrange wings. Broil 6 inches from heat 25 minutes or until browned, turning occasionally. Transfer to serving dish.

In small saucepan over medium heat, combine Tabasco, vinegar, and butter; drizzle evenly over wings.

Serve celery sticks and blue cheese dressing for dipping. Makes 24 appetizers.

Cheryl Brown, South Jackson Council (Book 3)

Olive Bites

25 pitted ripe green olives
2–3 tablespoons minced
  green onions
½ cup all-purpose flour
¼ teaspoon salt
⅛ teaspoon dry mustard

1 cup (4-ounces) shredded sharp
  Cheddar cheese
3 tablespoons butter or
  margarine, melted
1 teaspoon milk
1–2 drops Tabasco

Stuff olives with onions and set aside. Combine flour, salt, and mustard in a bowl. Mix in the cheese. Shape a spoonful of dough around each olive and place on a baking sheet. Bake at 400º for 10–12 minutes. Serve at once.

Jeanette Boyd, Gulf Coast Council (Book 1)

Chile Cheese Squares

1 (4-ounce) can chopped green
  chiles, drained
1 (8-ounce) package shredded
  Monterey Jack or sharp
  Cheddar cheese

1 cup Bisquick
1 cup light cream
4 eggs, beaten
¼ teaspoon salt
¼ cup chopped green olives

Lightly grease 11x13-inch pan. Sprinkle chiles and cheese in the bottom of the pan. In a bowl, combine Bisquick, cream, eggs, and salt. Make sure it is thoroughly blended. Pour over chiles and cheese. Sprinkle with chopped olives. Bake 30 minutes at 375° or until puffed, golden, and a skewer inserted comes out clean. Let stand for 10 minutes before cutting.

Joann R. Biddle, Jackson North Council (Book 2)

Hanky Pankies

1 pound ground beef
1 pound hot sausage
1 pound American cheese
  (or Velveeta)
1 teaspoon Worcestershire
1 teaspoon oregano

½ teaspoon salt
½ teaspoon garlic salt
Dash of pepper
Party rye bread or Melba
  rounds

Brown ground beef and sausage in skillet, stirring until crumbly and brown; drain. Add cheese and let melt on low heat, stirring constantly. Mix in seasonings. Spread on bread. Place on baking sheet and broil for 5 minutes or until bubbly. Yields 75–80 servings.

Beverly Smith (Book 3)

Diane's Sweet and Sour Smokies

1 cup firmly packed brown
  sugar
3 tablespoons flour
1 cup pineapple juice
½ cup apple cider vinegar

2 teaspoons dry mustard
1½ teaspoons soy sauce
2 pounds miniature smoke
  sausages

Combine all ingredients, except sausages. Bring to a boil. Add sausages and reduce temperature to simmer. Serve with toothpicks.

Helen Allen, Greenwood Council (Book 3)

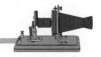

Meatballs

1 (32-ounce) jar grape jelly   1 pound bulk sausage
1 (16-ounce) jar barbeque sauce   Italian bread crumbs
2 pounds ground chuck

Melt grape jelly in crockpot. Add barbeque sauce. Mix last 3 ingredients together and roll into balls; brown; drain. Add to sauce and cook in crockpot on LOW for about 30 minutes, and keep hot.

Anna Earls, Greenwood Council (Book 3)

Cocktail Meatballs

MEATBALLS:

1 pound ground beef $\frac{1}{8}$ teaspoon pepper
1 egg, beaten   1 clove garlic, quartered
$\frac{1}{2}$ cup fine dry bread crumbs   2 teaspoons oil
1 teaspoon salt

Combine beef, egg, bread crumbs, salt, and pepper; shape into bite-size Meatballs. Over very low heat, sauté garlic in oil until pieces are tender, but not brown; discard garlic. Brown Meatballs on all sides; remove. Reserve 1 tablespoon fat.

SAUCE:

1 cup Coca Cola $\frac{1}{8}$ teaspoon black pepper
$\frac{1}{4}$ teaspoon dry mustard   1 tablespoon vinegar
2 tablespoons ketchup   1 tablespoon soy sauce

Add Sauce ingredients to reserved 1 tablespoon fat and bring to a boil. Add Meatballs; cook over low heat until most of Sauce is absorbed. Makes 40.

Beth Harbour, Meridian Council (Book 1)

Sausage Cheese Balls

2 pounds Jimmy Dean sausage, uncooked
1½ cups all-purpose biscuit mix
1 (16-ounce) package shredded sharp Cheddar cheese
½ cup finely chopped onion
½ cup finely chopped celery
½ teaspoon garlic powder

Preheat oven to 375º. Mix all ingredients. Form into 1-inch balls. Bake 15 minutes on ungreased cookie sheet until golden brown. Sausage cheese balls can be frozen uncooked. Makes about 6 dozen.

Note: For a firmer texture, add an extra 3 cups of biscuit mix and an extra 2 cups shredded cheese to the ingredients listed above.

Frances H. Welch, Mendenhall, MS (Book 4)

Coon Balls

Coon cheese was introduced to Australia in the early 1930's by Fred Walker from the Kraft Walker Cheese Company.

1 (8-ounce) package Coon cheese
1 pound bulk sausage
3½ cups Bisquick

Grate cheese and combine with sausage. Mix Bisquick into this and work all together well. Roll into small balls and bake at 325º for 13 minutes or until brown.

Ouva Green, Meridian Council; Jolene Baker, Gulf Coast Council; Dyphane O'Neal, Natchez Council; Joyce H. Smith, Jackson North Council (Book 1)

Chicken Cheese Ball

2 (8-ounce) packages cream
  cheese, softened
2 teaspoons instant chicken
  broth
3 green onions, chopped

2–3 shakes garlic or onion
  powder
1 (5-ounce) can cooked chicken,
  drained
Chopped pecans

Combine all ingredients, except pecans, and mix well. Shape into a ball and roll in chopped pecans.

Tommie Moore, Laurel, MS (Book 4)

Chicken Almond Spread

1 (3-ounce) package cream
  cheese, softened
½ teaspoon celery salt
½ teaspoon onion salt
1 teaspoon Worcestershire
Dash of Tabasco
⅓ cup sour cream

Snipped parsley
¼ cup finely chopped toasted
  almonds
½ cup finely chopped, cooked
  chicken
1 (4-ounce) can mushrooms,
  drained, finely chopped

Several hours or the day before serving, mix softened cream cheese with celery and onion salts, Worcestershire, Tabasco, sour cream, and parsley. Stir in almonds, chicken, and mushrooms. Mold in serving dish; refrigerate until chilled. Unmold spread and sprinkle with paprika. Serve with Melba toast rounds or crackers.

Willie Allen Williams, Clarksdale Club (Book 1)

Party Cheeseball

2 (8-ounce) packages cream
cheese, softened
1 (8-ounce) package shredded
sharp Cheddar cheese
1 tablespoon chopped pimento

1 teaspoon lemon juice
1 tablespoon grated onion
2 teaspoons Worcestershire
1 tablespoon chopped green
bell pepper

Combine softened cheese with the rest of the ingredients. Roll into a ball. Chill until serving.

Sweet Pea Dees, Jackson South Council (Book 2)

Dried Beef Log

1 (8-ounce) package cream
cheese, softened
1/4 cup grated Parmesan cheese
1 tablespoon prepared
horseradish

1/3 cup chopped pimento-stuffed
green olives
2 (4-ounce) jars dried beef,
finely snipped

Blend cream cheese, Parmesan, and horseradish. Stir in olives. On wax paper, roll ball in snipped beef. Wrap and chill several hours or overnight. Serve with crackers.

Bubbles Talbot, Gulf Coast Council (Book 2)

Cheese Ring

Rosalynn Carter spreads this mixture thin in a pie plate, tops it with straw-berry preserves, and serves it in wedges.

1 pound sharp Cheddar
  cheese, grated
1 cup finely chopped pecans
1 medium onion, grated

¼ teaspoon garlic powder
½ teaspoon Tabasco
¾ cup mayonnaise

Mix all ingredients in food processor. Press into lightly greased, 1-quart mold and chill. Unmold onto glass plate. Center may be filled with strawberry preserves.

Dorothy Smith, Meridian Council (Book 1)

Cucumber Nut Rolls

1 (8-ounce) package cream
  cheese, softened
1 teaspoon grated onion

2 teaspoons grated cucumber
⅓–½ cup finely chopped
  pecans

Cream together cream cheese, onion, and cucumber. Form into tiny balls and roll in nuts. Refrigerate. Serve.

Note: You can add the pecans to the mixture and spread on sandwiches to serve.

Beth Harbour, Meridian Council (Book 1)

Has any means of communication revolutionized the daily lives of ordinary people more than the telephone? Simply described, it is a system which converts sound, specifically the human voice, to electrical impulses of various frequencies and then back to a tone that sounds like the original voice.

Curry Dip

This is a great dip for fresh vegetables such as cauliflower, celery, carrot sticks, and bell pepper slices.

1 clove garlic, minced
2 cups mayonnaise
5 tablespoons ketchup
1 dash hot sauce
1½ teaspoons Worcestershire
2 tablespoons curry powder
½ teaspoon salt

Mix all ingredients together and chill for 1 hour before serving.

Diana M. Taylor, Jackson South Council; Carolyn Jacks,
Greenwood Council; Luna Pope, Columbus Club (Book 1)

Mother-in-Law's Hot Dip

2 (8-ounce) packages cream
  cheese, softened
2 cups shredded Swiss cheese
1 cup mayonnaise
1 pound bacon, fried and
  crumbled (do not use
  bacon bits), divided
1 bunch green onions, chopped

Mix together cream cheese, Swiss cheese, mayonnaise, half of the crumbled bacon, and green onions. Put in small baking dish, and top with remaining bacon. Bake at 350° for about 20 minutes or until bubbly hot. Serve with Wheat Thins.

Peggy Runnels, Mendenhall, MS (Book 3)

Jane's Broccoli Dip

1 stick margarine
1 cup chopped onion
2 (16-ounce) packages frozen, chopped broccoli
1 (4-ounce) can sliced mushrooms, drained
1 cup slivered almonds

1½ (9-ounce) rolls garlic cheese
2 (10¾-ounce) cans cream of mushroom soup
Tabasco to taste
Worcestershire to taste

Sauté onion in margarine. Add broccoli and simmer until tender. Add remaining ingredients and serve hot with corn chips. Makes 4 cups.

Mary V. Dunn, Meridian Council (Book 1)

Mississippi State Sin

1 loaf French bread
1½ cups sour cream
2 cups shredded Cheddar cheese
1 (8-ounce) package cream cheese, softened

⅓ cup chopped green onions
½ cup chopped ham
⅓ cup chopped green chiles
Dash of Worcestershire

Slice off top of bread and hollow out inside. Mix remaining ingredients. Pour into hollowed bread and place top back on bread. Wrap in foil. Bake at 350º for 1 hour. Serve as a dip with hollowed-out pieces of bread, crackers, or chips.

Donna R. Wade, Columbus, MS (Book 4)

Corn Dip

1 cup mayonnaise
2 (11-ounce) cans Mexicorn
1 pint sour cream
2 bunches green onions,
  chopped
1 teaspoon lemon juice
2 jalapeño peppers, chopped

2 cups grated mild Cheddar
  cheese
2 cups grated sharp Cheddar
  cheese
1 teaspoon Cajun seasoning
Chopped black olives (optional)

Mix all ingredients well. Chill. Serve with chips or crackers.

Irene S. Willard, Oxford, MS (Book 4)

Monterey Jack Salsa

1 (4-ounce) can chopped green
  chiles
1 (3¼-ounce) can chopped
  black olives
¼ pound Monterey Jack
  cheese, shredded

4 green onions, chopped
1 tomato, chopped
½ cup Zesty Italian salad
  dressing
¼ cup chopped cilantro
  (optional)

Mix all together and place on serving dish. Top with more grated Monterey Jack cheese. Serve with bite-size tortilla chips.

Betty Byrd, Jackson, MS (Book 4)

Ro-Tel Dip

1 pound ground beef	1 (10-ounce) can Ro-Tel tomatoes
1 pound American cheese	and chile peppers
½ teaspoon chili powder	2 teaspoons Worcestershire

Brown ground beef. Drain. Melt cheese into ground beef; add remaining ingredients. Serve warm with Fritos.

Debbie Wren, Jackson North Council (Book 1)

Texas Straw Hat

1 cup chopped onion	½ teaspoon pepper
⅔ cup chopped celery	2 (6-ounce) cans tomato paste
⅔ cup chopped bell pepper	2 cups water
3 tablespoons oil	2 teaspoons Worcestershire
2 pounds ground beef	Dash of Tabasco
2–3 teaspoons chili powder	2 (6-ounce) packages corn chips
2 teaspoons salt	2 cups shredded sharp
½ teaspoon thyme	Cheddar cheese

In large skillet, cook onion, celery, and bell pepper in oil until tender, but not brown. Add ground beef and brown slightly. Drain. Add remaining ingredients, except corn chips and cheese. Simmer uncovered for 1 hour, stirring occasionally. Serve the meaty sauce on corn chips topped with grated cheese. Makes 6–7 servings.

Wendall B. Sanford, Hattiesburg Council (Book 2)

Tex Mex Dip

1 (16-ounce) can refried beans
3 medium-ripe avocados,
   mashed, or use frozen
   guacamole dip
2 tablespoons lemon juice
½ teaspoon salt
¼ teaspoon pepper
1 cup sour cream
½ cup mayonnaise
1 (1.25-ounce) package taco
   seasoning mix

1 large bunch green onions,
   chopped (approximately
   1 cup)
3 tomatoes, chopped
2 (3½-ounce) cans pitted ripe
   olives
1 (8-ounce) package shredded
   Cheddar cheese
Large round tortilla chips

FIRST LAYER:

Spread refried beans on a large shallow serving platter.

SECOND LAYER:

Combine avocados or dip with lemon juice, salt, and pepper; spread over First Layer.

THIRD LAYER:

Combine sour cream, mayonnaise, and taco mix; spread over Second Layer.

FOURTH LAYER:

Sprinkle with green onions, tomatoes, and olives. Cover with grated cheese. Serve with tortilla chips. Enjoy!

Variation: Sprinkle with minced garlic and chopped jalapeño peppers.

Nelda McMullan, Kyla Moore, Margaret Louise Collier, Ocean Springs, MS (Book 4)

Almond-Bacon Cheese Dip

⅓ cup sliced almonds
3 strips bacon
1 tablespoon chopped green
  onions, including tops

¼ pound cheese, finely grated
½ cup (or more) mayonnaise
½ teaspoon salt

Chop almonds fine. Fry bacon crisp; drain and crumble. Combine all ingredients and mix. Add more mayonnaise, if desired. Refrigerate until served. Serve with chicken-flavored crackers.

Betty Staples, Laurel, MS (Book 4)

Artichoke-Crab Dip or Spread

1 (15-ounce) can artichokes
  (not marinated type)
1 cup mayonnaise

1 cup grated Parmesan cheese
1 (7.5-ounce) can crabmeat,
  drained

Drain, quarter, and mash artichokes. Add mayonnaise, cheese, and crabmeat. Bake at 350º for 20–30 minutes. Sprinkle with paprika and serve hot with crackers.

Note: You can substitute 8 ounces cream cheese for mayonnaise or use 2 (15-ounce) cans of artichokes and leave out the crabmeat.

Mary Roy Williams, Cleveland, MS (Book 4)

Trophy-Winning Spinach Dip

1 (10-ounce) package frozen, chopped spinach, thawed and drained
1 (16-ounce) carton sour cream
1 cup Hellmann's mayonnaise
1 (8-ounce) can water chestnuts, drained and chopped (optional)
3 green onions, chopped
1 (1.4-ounce) package vegetable soup mix
1 large, unsliced oval or round loaf bread, hollowed out (optional)

In medium bowl, stir all ingredients until well mixed. Cover; chill 2 hours to blend flavors. Stir before serving. If desired, spoon dip into hollowed-out bread.

Barbara Staples, Laurel, MS (Book 4)

Pimento and Cheese

1 pound sharp Cheddar cheese, grated
1 (8-ounce) package cream cheese, softened
1 large jar pimentos, drained
¾ cup (or more) mayonnaise
Black pepper to taste
1 teaspoon garlic salt
1 teaspoon red pepper
Salt and pepper to taste

Combine cheeses and pimento; add other ingredients. Whip with mixer. May need to add more mayonnaise. Store in refrigerator. Great with celery stalks, crackers, or as an open-faced sandwich appetizer.

Linda Morphis, Meridian Council (Book 2)

Shrimp Dip

This can be made two days ahead.

1 (8-ounce) carton sour cream
1 (8-ounce) package cream
  cheese, softened
½ cup chopped celery
½ cup chopped onion

Red pepper to taste
Juice of 1 lemon
Salt and black pepper to taste
2 (4½-ounce) cans shrimp,
  drained

Mix sour cream and cream cheese until smooth. Fold in celery and onion; add red pepper, lemon juice, salt and black pepper. Mash shrimp with a fork and add to mixture.

Mary S. Shoemake, Natchez Council (Book 1)

Shrimp Dip

¼ cup milk
1 (8-ounce) package cream
  cheese, softened
1 (4½-ounce) can shrimp,
  deveined, rinsed, drained,
  and chopped

1 teaspoon lemon juice
1 teaspoon Worcestershire
½ teaspoon garlic salt
2 tablespoons mayonnaise or
  Miracle Whip
4 ounces garlic cheese spread

Blend milk gradually into cream cheese. Stir in shrimp, lemon juice, Worcestershire, garlic salt, mayonnaise, and cheese spread. Cover; refrigerate at least 1 hour.

Clora Harris, Natchez Council (Book 2)

Crab-Stuffed Eggs

12 hard-boiled eggs, halved
lengthwise
1 (6½-ounce) can crabmeat,
drained and flaked
2 tablespoons melted butter
2–3 tablespoons mayonnaise

4 teaspoons grated onion
½ teaspoon salt
¼ cup sour cream
4 drops Tabasco
½ teaspoon Worcestershire
⅛ teaspoon white pepper

Remove egg yolks from whites; sieve yolks; toss with crabmeat. Blend in remaining ingredients. Stuff egg whites with mixture. Garnish each with pimiento or parsley.

Jeanette Boyd, Gulf Coast Council (Book 2)

Extra Special Stuffed Eggs

1 dozen hard-boiled eggs
1 (3-ounce) can deviled ham
½ tablespoon white vinegar
½ tablespoon celery salt

Pepper to taste
2 tablespoons chopped sweet
pickles
Mayonnaise

Peel and halve eggs. Remove yolks to a bowl. Add remaining ingredients to yolks and mix well; fill egg white halves with yolk mixture.

Sandy Harrell, Jackson North Council (Book 2)

Calcutta Fruit Sauce

1 (8-ounce) carton sour cream
⅓ cup orange marmalade
1 teaspoon lemon or lime juice
½ teaspoon curry powder
¼ teaspoon ginger

Combine all ingredients and serve over chilled fruits, such as melon balls, bananas, strawberries, or pineapple chunks.

Helen Graham, Jackson Council (Book 3)

Jezebel Sauce

1 cup apple jelly
1 cup peach preserves
1 cup pineapple preserves
Horseradish to taste
Dry mustard to taste

Mix jelly and preserves. Add horseradish and dry mustard to taste. Great with ham; can also be served with poultry or fish.

Mable Guarr, Meridian Council (Book 2)

Strawberry Fig Jam

3 cups mashed figs (cut off
   both ends)
3 cups sugar
1 (5-ounce) or 2 (3-ounce)
   packages strawberry Jell-O

Combine all, and cook 7 minutes after it comes to a rolling boil. Pour into sterilized jars and seal.

Marie McCall, Natchez Council (Book 1)

Pepper Jelly

½ cup hot peppers
1½ cups apple cider vinegar,
   divided
6 cups sugar

¾ cup chopped bell peppers
3¼ teaspoons salt
1 (6-ounce) bottle Certo
Food coloring (red or green)

Put peppers and 1 cup vinegar in blender on liquefy for at least 30 seconds. Rinse blender with remaining ½ cup vinegar. Put sugar, bell peppers, and remaining ½ cup vinegar in large pot; add salt. Bring to a hard boil for 1 minute. Remove from heat for 10 minutes. Add Certo and food coloring. Boil for 1 minute more. Pour into 6 small jars.

Bernadine Bratton, Tupelo Council (Book 1)

Champagne Jelly

Ideal for party favors.

3 cups sugar
2 cups pink champagne

1 (3-ounce) package liquid
   pectin

Combine sugar and champagne in a large Dutch oven. Cook over medium heat, stirring, until sugar dissolves (do not boil). Remove from heat; stir in liquid pectin. Skim off foam with a metal spoon. Quickly pour hot jelly into hot sterilized jars, leaving ¼ inch of head space. Wipe jars; put on metal lids and screw on bands. Process in boiling water bath for 5 minutes. Let stand for 8 hours for jelly to set up. Yields 5 half pints.

Angela L. McCoy, Jackson Council (Book 3)

Mary's T.V. Trash

1 (12-ounce) box Corn Chex
1 (10-ounce) box Cherrios
1 (¾-pound) bag pretzel sticks
1 (24-ounce) can cocktail
  peanuts
1 pound shelled pecans

1 cup bacon grease
1 cup Worcestershire
1 teaspoon onion salt
1 teaspoon celery salt
1 teaspoon seasoning salt

Place Chex, Cheerios, pretzels, peanuts, and pecans in a large roasting pan. In a medium saucepan, melt bacon grease, Worcestershire, and salts. Pour this mixture over dry ingredients; stir well. Bake in 250º oven 1½ hours. Stir every 15 minutes.

Mary I. Smith (Book 3)

Nuts and Bolts

3 sticks margarine, melted
2 tablespoons garlic powder
2 tablespoons garlic salt
1 teaspoon celery salt
3 tablespoons Worcestershire
1¼ teaspoons cayenne pepper

1 (12-ounce) box Corn Chex
1 (10-ounce) box Cheerios
1 (12-ounce) box Rice Chex
1 (8-ounce) box pretzels
1 quart pecans
1 quart Spanish peanuts

Mix first 6 ingredients and set aside. Mix dry cereals, pretzels, and pecans together. Slowly pour the margarine mixture over the dry mixture, tossing gently to make sure all dry ingredients are coated. Cook at 200º in a large baking pan for 2 hours, stirring every 15 minutes. Add peanuts the last 15 minutes. Empty on paper bag to cool before storing in jars.

Jess Buford, Jackson South Council (Book 1)

Oyster Crackers Snack

1 (16-ounce) package unsalted
  oyster crackers
1 (0.7-ounce) package original
  ranch dressing mix

¾ teaspoon garlic salt
2 teaspoons dill weed
¾ cup Wesson oil

Place crackers in large bowl. Mix dry ingredients and sprinkle over crackers. Drizzle oil over crackers. Stir many times with rubber spatula until oil is absorbed. Freezes well.

Beth F. Fike (Book 3)

Cheese Straws

2 cups flour
2 sticks margarine
1 teaspoon salt

1 (8-ounce) package shredded
  extra sharp Cheddar cheese
Hot sauce to taste

Mix all ingredients together. Put through cookie press (star disk) onto cookie sheet. Place in 300º preheated oven until golden brown.

Winsel Walker, Laurel, MS (Book 4)

Toasted Buttered Pecans

½ pound (about 2 cups)
  pecan halves

1½ teaspoons seasoned salt
2 teaspoons butter or margarine

Spread pecans evenly in a shallow baking pan. Sprinkle with seasoned salt and dot with butter. Bake at 325º for 25 minutes, stirring frequently. Makes 2 cups.

Eurcle Culipher, Jackson North Council (Book 2)

Bread and Breakfast

1878
Butterstamp

The first telephone with a combined receiver-transmitter that could be held in the hand looked like a butterstamp—hence its name. You talked into one end, turned the instrument around, and listened to the other end. The push button signaled the operator. This model was in service when the world's first commercial switchboard opened in New Haven, Connecticut, in 1878. Western Union opened the first large city exchange in San Francisco that same year. The public switched telephone network was born; no longer limited to people on the same wire, folks could now talk to many others on different lines.

Icebox Rolls

1 egg
1 (¼-ounce) package yeast
2 cups lukewarm water

½ cup Wesson oil
½ cup sugar
6–7 cups all-purpose flour

Mix all ingredients together with enough flour to make a stiff dough. Let rise in warm place for 1½ hours; work dough and put in refrigerator. Use as needed. Let rise 30–40 minutes before baking. Bake at 400° for about 15 minutes.

Jean Walker, Hattiesburg Council (Book 1)

Rolls

1 (¼-ounce) package yeast
¼ cup lukewarm water
½ cup sugar
½ cup oil

2 eggs
1 teaspoon salt
1 cup warm water
4 cups all-purpose flour

Dissolve yeast in ¼ cup lukewarm water. Mix with remaining ingredients in large bowl. Let rise about 4 hours or overnight.

Separate into 3 lumps. Roll each one and cut into 8 slices. Roll from wide end into a crescent. Place on baking sheet and let rise at least 4 hours. Bake at 400º until brown.

Blanche Maxwell, McComb Club (Book 1)

Angel Biscuits

1 (¼-ounce) package yeast
¼ cup lukewarm water
2 cups all-purpose flour
2 tablespoons sugar
1 teaspoon salt

1 teaspoon baking powder
½ teaspoon baking soda
3 tablespoons shortening
½ cup buttermilk

Soften yeast in water and set aside. Sift dry ingredients together. Cut shortening into dry ingredients. Add buttermilk and softened yeast. Stir until well blended. Store in refrigerator for 1 hour. Roll out and cut biscuits ½ inch thick and 2 inches wide. Let rise 1 hour. Bake at 425º for 10 minutes.

Beth Harbour, Meridian Council; Joan Wade, Jackson South Council (Book 1)

Popeye's Biscuits

1 stick butter, softened
4 cups Bisquick
¾ cup club soda

1 (8-ounce) container sour
  cream

Cut butter into Bisquick. Mix with remaining ingredients. Roll out dough on aluminum foil coated with flour and cut with a glass. Bake at 400º for 15 minutes.

Mignyon Bouchard, Silver Creek, MS (Book 4)

Three-Ingredient Biscuits

2 cups self-rising flour
1 cup butter, melted

1 (8-ounce) container sour cream

Stir ingredients together just until blended. Spoon batter into lightly greased muffin tins, filling about half full. Bake in preheated 350° oven for about 25 minutes, or until lightly browned.

Nina G. Kimbriel, Lake Village, AR (Book 4)

Easy Cornbread

1 tablespoon shortening
¾ cup cornmeal
1 tablespoon self-rising flour

½ tablespoon sugar
½ cup milk
1 egg, beaten

Preheat oven to 425°. Place shortening in small black skillet. Place skillet into preheated oven to melt shortening, about 7 minutes. Mix together cornmeal, flour, and sugar. Stir in milk and egg. Immediately pour or spoon batter into skillet and bake 20–25 minutes. Cornbread should fall out of skillet easily after baking.

Janet Dukes, Jackson North Council (Book 1)

Fancy Cornbread

1 cup cornmeal
1 (7-ounce) can cream-style
   corn
⅓ (4-ounce) can chile peppers
½ cup grated Parmesan cheese
1 medium onion, chopped
1 tablespoon baking powder

¾ cup buttermilk
⅓ cup shortening or bacon
   grease
2 eggs, beaten
½ teaspoon salt
½ teaspoon baking soda

Mix all ingredients and bake in a greased, hot skillet at 375° for 20–25 minutes.

Ila Knott, Capitol Life Member Council (Book 1)

Broccoli Cornbread

1 (10-ounce) package frozen
  chopped broccoli
1 cup grated sharp cheese
1 onion, chopped
4 eggs, beaten

1 teaspoon salt
¼ cup buttermilk
1 (8½-ounce) package Jiffy
  cornbread mix
1 stick butter, melted

Cook broccoli according to package directions; drain. Mix with next 5 ingredients. Then add cornbread mix and melted butter. Grease a 9x13-inch pan and bake at 375º for 25–30 minutes.

Fredonia Granholm, Tupelo Council (Book 3)

Sausage Upside-Down Cornbread

1 pound bulk sausage
1 cup chopped onion
⅓ cup chopped bell pepper
2 tablespoons flour
1 (6-ounce) can tomato paste
1 teaspoon salt
1 teaspoon chili powder

⅛ teaspoon pepper
4 ounces (1 cup) Cheddar cheese,
  cut in ½-inch cubes
½ cup pitted ripe olives, sliced
2 (8½-ounce) packages corn
  muffin mix

Preheat oven to 400º. Cook sausage, onion, and bell pepper in a skillet until sausage is brown and crumbly. Stir in flour. Mix in tomato paste, salt, chili powder, and pepper. Remove from heat and stir in cheese and olives. Spread evenly in a 9-inch square pan, sprayed with vegetable spray. Prepare muffin mix according to package directions; spread over sausage. Bake 30–35 minutes. Let stand in pan 5 minutes; loosen edges. Invert onto plate. Serve immediately.

Betty Staples, Laurel, MS (Book 4)

Sweet Potato Cornbread

2 tablespoons plus ⅓ cup
  vegetable oil, divided
1 cup mashed sweet potatoes
3 eggs

1½ cups milk or buttermilk
2½ cups self-rising cornmeal
½ cup sugar

Preheat oven to 375º. Add 2 tablespoons oil to cast-iron skillet, and preheat for 10 minutes. Combine sweet potatoes, eggs, and milk in large bowl. Blend until smooth. Add remaining ⅓ cup oil, cornmeal, and sugar. Stir until combined. Pour batter into skillet. Bake 45–50 minutes until golden brown.

Kate Rutherford, Jackson, MS (Book 4)

Cornbread Dressing Balls

1 (10- to 12-ounce) package
  cornbread mix
½ cup butter or margarine,
  melted, divided
1½ cups chopped celery
1 cup chopped onion
¼ cup chopped parsley

½ teaspoon rubbed sage
½ teaspoon dried thyme leaves
1 teaspoon salt
¼ teaspoon pepper
1 egg
½ (10-ounce) can clear chicken
  broth, undiluted

Make and bake cornbread as package directs; cool in pan or on wire rack 25 minutes. Crumble baked cornbread into medium mixing bowl. Preheat oven to 325º. Heat ¼ cup butter in medium skillet; add celery, onion, and parsley. Sauté, stirring until celery and onion are tender, about 5 minutes. Add to crumbled cornbread along with sage, thyme, salt, pepper, egg, and chicken broth; mix well. With hands, lightly form mixture into balls, using about ½ cup for each. Arrange in greased, shallow baking dish. Brush with remaining butter and bake covered for 30 minutes. Remove cover; bake 15 minutes longer or until browned on top.

Note: Dressing balls may be baked in the oven with a turkey.

Mrs. John (Safronia) Ballard, Columbus Club (Book 1)

Mississippi Hush Puppies

1 cup self-rising cornmeal mix
½ cup self-rising flour
1 tablespoon sugar
1 large egg, slightly beaten
½ cup milk or beer*

½ cup diced onion
½ cup chopped green bell
   pepper
1 jalapeño pepper, seeded and
   chopped

Combine first 3 ingredients in a large bowl; make a well in center of mixture. In the well, add egg and remaining ingredients, stirring until moistened. Pour oil to a depth of 3 inches into a Dutch oven or heavy saucepan and heat to 375°. Drop batter by rounded tablespoonfuls into oil and fry in batches, 2 minutes on each side or until golden brown. Drain on paper towels; serve immediately. Makes 1½ dozen.

*Substituting beer for milk makes these puppies lighter and tangier.

Barbara Staples, Laurel, MS (Book 4)

Hush Puppies

½ cup cornmeal
½ cup all-purpose flour
1 tablespoon sugar
1 teaspoon baking powder

½ teaspoon salt
1 small onion, chopped fine
1 egg
Beer, as required

Mix cornmeal, flour, sugar, baking powder, and salt together. Add onion mixed with egg. Mix with enough beer to make a thick paste. Deep-fry in hot oil by dropping with teaspoon. Fry until brown.

Mildred Hudson, Capitol Life Member Club (Book 1)

Squash Puppies

5 medium yellow squash
1 egg, beaten
½ cup buttermilk
1 medium onion, chopped

¾ cup self-rising cornmeal
½ cup self-rising flour
Salt and pepper to taste

Cook squash in water to cover; drain, mash, and drain again. Combine all other ingredients and mix with squash. Drop by scant tablespoonfuls in hot oil. Cook until golden brown. Drain on paper towels. Serve hot.

Beth Harbour, Meridian, MS (Book 4)

Amish Friendship Bread

STARTER:
1 cup all-purpose flour
1 cup sugar

1 cup milk

Combine flour, sugar, and milk in a glass mixer bowl and stir with a wooden spoon. Do not refrigerate. Place mixture in Ziploc bag and let stand at room temperature for a day. The next day, begin instructions for Day 1.

DAY 1 through DAY 5:
Each day, squeeze the bag and expel the air.

DAY 6:
1 cup all-purpose flour
1 cup sugar

1 cup milk

Add flour, sugar, and milk; mix well by squeezing the bag.

DAY 7 through DAY 9:
Each day, squeeze the bag.

(continued)

(Amish Friendship Bread continued)

DAY 10:

1 cup all-purpose flour	1 cup milk
1 cup sugar	

Place the batter from the plastic bag in a large bowl. Add flour, sugar, and milk. Mix well with a wooden spoon. Place 1 cup batter in each of 23 large plastic bags and give to friends along with the instructions. Should have about 2 cups remaining.

MIXTURE 1:

¾ cup oil	2 teaspoons vanilla extract
3 eggs	

With leftover starter (about 2 cups), add oil, eggs, and vanilla. Mix well.

MIXTURE 2:

2 cups all-purpose flour	½ teaspoon baking soda
1 cup sugar	1 cup chopped walnuts or
1½ teaspoons baking powder	pecans
½ teaspoon salt	Dried cranberries (optional)
2 teaspoons cinnamon	Cinnamon and sugar for
1 (5-ounce) box vanilla instant	sprinkling
pudding mix	

In separate bowl, mix flour, sugar, baking powder, salt, cinnamon, pudding mix, baking soda, and nuts. (I add a few dried cranberries to mine.) Spray 2 loaf pans with nonstick cooking spray. Combine Mixtures 1 and 2. Pour ½ into each loaf pan. Sprinkle cinnamon and sugar on top of batter. Bake at 325º for an hour; test with a toothpick for doneness. If batter sticks to toothpick, cook about 10 minutes longer, then check again. Freezes well.

Margie Sasser, Edwards, MS (Book 4)

Jewish Bread

No milk is used in this recipe.

4 eggs
3½ cups brown sugar
2 cups self-rising flour

1 teaspoon vanilla extract
1–2 cups chopped pecans

Preheat oven to 325°. Mix eggs and brown sugar to form thick mixture. Pour in heavy boiler and heat over low heat until sugar melts completely. Continue heating, and add flour and vanilla. Remove from heat and add nuts. Pour into greased 9x10-inch cake pan and bake for 30 minutes. As soon as toothpick comes clean, remove from oven and cool completely before cutting. It will have the consistency of a brownie.

Becky Hilderbrand, Pearl, MS (Book 4)

Zucchini Nut Bread

2 cups sugar
1 cup Wesson oil
2 cups grated zucchini
3 cups all-purpose flour
1 teaspoon salt
1 teaspoon cinnamon

1 teaspoon baking soda
¼ teaspoon baking powder
3 eggs
3 tablespoons vanilla
½ cup chopped nuts

Mix sugar, oil, and zucchini. In separate bowl, mix flour, salt, cinnamon, baking soda, and baking powder. Beat eggs until light and foamy. Add vanilla, then zucchini mixture to eggs. Add flour mixture to egg mixture; blend and add nuts. Divide batter into 2 greased and floured loaf pans. Bake at 350° for 1 hour. Remove from pans at once and cool on rack. Good to wrap in aluminum foil and freeze.

Thelma Poche, Jackson North Council (Book 2)

Banana Bread

1 cup butter
2 cups sugar
4 eggs
6 bananas, mashed
4 cups all-purpose flour

2 teaspoons baking soda
2 cups nuts
2 cups raisins
1 tablespoon vanilla extract

Cream butter and sugar together; add eggs, one at a time. Then add mashed bananas, flour, and baking soda; mix well. Add nuts, raisins, and vanilla. Pour into 2 greased loaf pans and bake at 350º for 30–40 minutes. Makes 2 loafs.

Lynette Ford, Jackson South Council (Book 1)

Fresh Apple Loaf

2 cups sugar
1 cup oil
2 eggs, well beaten
3 cups self-rising flour
3 cups shredded or finely
  chopped peeled apples

1 cup dark raisins
1 cup chopped pecans
2 teaspoons vanilla extract
1 (10-ounce) jar maraschino
  cherries, cut up

Cream sugar and oil; add eggs. Then add flour and mix well. Add apples, raisins, pecans, vanilla, and cherries. Pour into 2 well-greased loaf pans. Bake at 300º for 55 minutes or until done.

Martha Springs, Jackson South Council (Book 1)

Strawberry Bread

3 cups sifted all-purpose flour
1 teaspoon baking soda
1 teaspoon salt
2–3 teaspoons cinnamon
2 cups sugar
4 eggs, beaten

1¼ cups vegetable oil
2 cups sliced strawberries, or
  2 (10-ounce) packages frozen,
  sliced strawberries, thawed
1 cup chopped pecans

Preheat oven to 325º. Sift dry ingredients together. Mix eggs, oil, strawberries, and nuts. Add to dry ingredients, stirring just enough to moisten. Pour into 2 greased loaf pans. Bake for 45–50 minutes or until done. Cool in pans before removing. Freezes well. Flavor improves if loaves are wrapped and allowed to set overnight.

Christine Gaskin, Laurel, MS (Book 4)

Cranberry Nut Bread

⅔ cup shortening
1⅓ cups sugar
3 eggs
3 cups mashed bananas
  (approximately 4)
3½ cups all-purpose flour,
  sifted

4 teaspoons baking powder
¾ teaspoon salt
½ teaspoon baking soda
1 cup chopped nuts
1 (16-ounce) can (1¾ cups)
  whole berry cranberry sauce

Cream shortening and sugar thoroughly. Add eggs and beat well. Stir in mashed bananas. Sift together dry ingredients and gradually add to mixture. Stir in nuts; fold in cranberry sauce. Pour into greased and floured loaf pan. Bake at 300º for 45–65 minutes.

Mrs. F. L. "Flo" Upton, Jackson North Council (Book 2)

Orange Bread

1 cup orange peel, cut in
  fine strips
2 cups sugar, divided
2 eggs
1 cup sweet milk

3 tablespoons butter, melted
Dash of salt
3½ cups all-purpose flour
3 teaspoons baking powder
1 cup chopped nuts

Cook orange peel in water until tender and drain. Add 1 cup sugar and cook until syrupy; let cool. Beat eggs well; add remaining 1 cup sugar and milk; beat again. Add melted butter, salt, flour, and baking powder; add cold orange peel mixture. Add nuts. Bake in 2 greased loaf pans at 350º for 50–60 minutes or until done.

Rubye Nash, Corinth Club (Book 1)

Sweet Potato Bread

1 cup margarine, softened
3 cups sugar
3 eggs
1 teaspoon vanilla
2 cups baked mashed sweet
  potatoes

3 cups all-purpose flour
1½ teaspoons baking soda
½ teaspoon baking powder
1½ teaspoons cinnamon
1 teaspoon ground cloves
½ teaspoon ground nutmeg

Preheat oven to 350º. Cream margarine and sugar. Beat in eggs and vanilla. Add mashed sweet potatoes. Sift together the flour, salt, baking soda, baking powder, and spices. Blend with sweet potato mixture. Bake in 2 greased and floured loaf pans for 60–65 minutes. Let stand 10 minutes. Remove and cool on racks. Wrap and store overnight. Makes 2 loaves.

Note: You may add 1 cup chopped pecans and 1 cup raisins, or 1 cup Bran Buds and ½ cup chopped dates before baking.

George Ann Miller, Jackson South Council (Book 1)

Blueberry Muffins

⅔ cup shortening
1 cup sugar
3 eggs
3 cups all-purpose flour
3 heaping teaspoons baking
  powder

1 teaspoon salt
1 cup milk
1 (10-ounce) can blueberries,
  drained

Cream shortening and sugar until fluffy; add eggs, one at a time, beating after each. Sift flour, baking powder, and salt. Add alternately with milk to egg mixture; beat well. Add blueberries; stir until well mixed. Bake in greased muffin tins at 375º for 15–20 minutes until done.

Shirley Clanton, Natchez Council (Book 1)

Pecan Pie Mini Muffins

1 cup packed brown sugar
½ cup all-purpose flour
1 cup chopped pecans

⅔ cup butter, melted
  (no substitutes)
2 eggs, beaten

In a bowl, combine brown sugar, flour, and pecans; set aside. Combine butter and eggs; mix well. Stir into flour mixture just until moist. Fill greased and floured (or paper-lined) miniature muffin tins ⅔ full. Bake at 350º for 10–15 minutes or until tests done. Remove immediately to cool on wire racks. Makes about 2 dozen mini muffins.

Evelyn Necaise, Kiln, MS (Book 4)

Orange Breakfast Ring

1 cup sugar
3 tablespoons grated orange
  rind

2 (12-ounce) cans refrigerated
  buttermilk biscuits
⅓ cup margarine, melted

Combine sugar and orange rind. Separate biscuits; dip each in melted margarine, then in sugar-orange mixture. Stand biscuits on sides, overlapping edges in greased 9-inch tube pan. Bake at 350º for 20 minutes or until golden brown. Remove ring from pan and invert on serving platter.

ICING:

1 (3-ounce) package cream
  cheese, softened

½ cup powdered sugar
2 tablespoons orange juice

Combine cream cheese and powdered sugar. Mix well until smooth. Add orange juice. Stir well. Spoon Icing over top of ring while hot.

Betty Staples, Laurel, MS (Book 4)

Monkey Bread

3 (10-count) cans biscuits
1 cup sugar
3 tablespoons cinnamon
1 cup chopped walnuts
  or pecans

1½ sticks margarine
1 cup brown sugar

Cut each biscuit into 4 pieces. Mix sugar and cinnamon. Roll biscuit pieces in sugar-cinnamon mixture; arrange in Bundt pan. Sprinkle nuts on top. Melt butter and stir in brown sugar. Pour over biscuits and nuts. Bake at 350º for 30 minutes.

Ruth J. McCormick, Capitol Life Member Club (Book 1)

Plucking Bread

This bread is eaten by "plucking" pieces off.

6 cups all-purpose flour,
  sifted, divided
½ cup sugar
1 teaspoon salt
2 cups milk, divided
1 (¼-ounce) package yeast

2 eggs, slightly beaten
1½ sticks butter or margarine
¼ cup butter, melted
2 cups sugar mixed with
  2 tablespoons cinnamon
1 cup chopped pecans

To 3 cups flour, add ½ cup sugar and salt; resift. Scald milk and cool to lukewarm. Measure ½ cup milk and stir in yeast. Stir eggs and 1½ sticks butter into remaining milk until butter is melted. Combine with flour mixture and yeast mixture; stir well (will look like thick syrup). Cover with towel and let rise 1½ hours. Stir in remaining 3 cups flour and refrigerate overnight.

Grease large tube pan. Turn dough onto floured board and form balls (smaller than ping pong balls). Dip each ball in melted butter and then in cinnamon-sugar mixture. (It's easier to forms balls first and work with small amounts of cinnamon-sugar mixture.) Sprinkle layer of chopped nuts in bottom of pan, then alternate layers of dough balls and pecans in pan. Bake in 350º oven for 55 minutes. Cool in pan for 15 minutes; turn onto large plate.

Evelyn Morgan, Jackson North Council (Book 2)

Sour Cream Coffee Cake

TOPPING:

½ cup chopped pecans
½ cup white or brown sugar

¼ cup cinnamon
2 teaspoons cocoa

Mix and set aside.

COFFEE CAKE:

1 (18¼-ounce) Duncan Hines butter cake mix
1 (3-ounce) package vanilla instant pudding mix

1 (8-ounce) carton sour cream
½ cup cooking oil
4 eggs

Combine cake mix and pudding mix; add sour cream and oil. Beat thoroughly. Add eggs, one at a time. Beat at least 7 minutes. Pour ⅓ of the batter into a greased and floured Bundt or tube pan. Add ⅓ of the Topping. Repeat layers twice, ending with Topping. Bake at 325º for 1 hour or until done. Let cool in pan at least 30 minutes after removing from oven.

Jo Herring, Jackson North Council (Book 2)

Waffles

1 egg
1⅓ cups buttermilk
1⅓ cups all-purpose flour
½ teaspoon baking powder

Dash of salt
⅛ cup oil
¼ teaspoon baking soda
1 teaspoon vanilla extract

Mix all ingredients together and pour in a hot waffle iron. This makes one batch of 4 squares.

Billie Buford, Oakland, MS (Book 4)

Doughnuts

2 cups Bisquick baking mix
2 tablespoons sugar
¼ cup milk
1 egg

1 teaspoon vanilla
¼ teaspoon cinnamon
¼ teaspoon nutmeg

Mix all ingredients in order, until smooth. Gently smooth dough into a ball on floured, cloth-covered board. Knead 8–10 times. Roll dough ¼ inch thick and cut with floured doughnut cutter. Heat fat or oil (3–4 inches) to 375º in deep fat fryer or kettle. Drop rings into hot oil. Fry about ½ minute on each side, until golden brown; drain. Makes 10–12 doughnuts.

Variation: For chocolate doughnuts, add ¼ cup cocoa with baking mix; increase sugar to ¼ cup and milk to ½ cup; omit cinnamon and nutmeg.

Mary Branch, Tupelo Council (Book 2)

Grits Casserole

1 cup grits
1 teaspoon salt
4 cups water
1 stick butter
¼ pound Velveeta cheese, cubed

¼ pound sharp Cheddar cheese, grated
3 eggs, slightly beaten
⅓ cup milk

Cook grits in salted water until done. Add butter, cheeses, eggs, and milk. Stir until melted and smooth. Place in greased 1½-quart casserole and bake at 325º–350º for 1 hour. May be made ahead of time and frozen until ready to use. Serves 6–8.

Fleta Boteler, Capitol Life Member Club, and Dot Bonner,
Natchez Council (Book 1)

Baked Grits

1 cup quick-cooking grits
1 teaspoon salt
4 cups boiling water
1 (4-ounce) roll smoked garlic
  cheese

1 stick margarine
2 eggs
Dash of garlic powder
½ cup cornflake crumbs

Cook grits in salted boiling water until done. Add garlic cheese and margarine; stir until melted. Beat eggs and add enough water to make 1 cup; pour into grits. Add garlic powder and pour into casserole dish. Top with cornflake crumbs. Bake at 350º for 45 minutes.

Ouva Green, Life Member, Meridian Council (Book 2)

Man-Size Omelet

2 teaspoons butter
3 large eggs
1 teaspoon milk
1 teaspoon grated Parmesan
  cheese
⅓ cup grated mozzarella
  cheese
⅓ cup grated sharp Cheddar
  cheese

1 slice precooked ham, cut in
  25 small squares
4 slices bacon, cooked crisp
1 teaspoon dry minced green
  onion
6 fresh mushrooms, sliced and
  sautéed
Salt and pepper to taste

Grease omelet pan with butter. Preheat on medium-low heat and keep at that temperature. Whip eggs with milk and Parmesan cheese, then pour in skillet. When eggs are manageable (nearly set) in the skillet, pour grated mozzarella and Cheddar across middle of eggs. Add squares of ham and bits of bacon. Sprinkle minced onion and slices of mushrooms over middle. Season to taste. Fold each side of eggs over the middle until secure. Slide out of pan onto plate for a delicious meal.

Ray Bryant, Jackson South Council (Book 1)

Creamed Eggs

¼ cup butter or margarine
1 teaspoon grated onion
3 tablespoons flour
1 teaspoon salt

⅛ teaspoon ground pepper
2 cups milk
6 hard-boiled eggs, sliced or
chopped

Melt butter and add grated onion, flour, and seasonings. Blend well and cook over low heat until bubbly. Add milk all at once; cook, stirring constantly, until thickened. Add boiled eggs and heat thoroughly. Serve hot on toast.

Brenda Beck, Tupelo Council (Book 1)

Breakfast Casserole

1 pound bulk sausage
½ stick butter or margarine,
  melted
6 slices white bread, crusts
  removed
1½ cups shredded Longhorn
  cheese

5 eggs, beaten well with mixer
2 cups half-and-half
1 teaspoon salt
1 teaspoon dry mustard

Cook sausage well, then drain. Melt butter in 9x13-inch Pyrex pan. Tear bread into small pieces and sprinkle over butter. Sprinkle drained sausage over bread. Sprinkle cheese over sausage. Beat eggs and remaining ingredients; pour over cheese. Chill for 8 hours or overnight. Bake at 350º for 40–50 minutes.

Nancy Alford, Jackson South Council and Frankie Miller,
Greenwood Council (Book 1)

Poor Man's Breakfast

12 ounces bacon, fried and crumbled

2½ tablespoons bacon grease

1 small onion, halved and sliced thin

3 medium potatoes, peeled and sliced thin

Salt and pepper to taste

6 eggs, beaten

Fry bacon and set aside. In bacon grease, sauté onion till clear. Add potatoes and seasoning. Cover; cook on low till potatoes are done. Add bacon back to mixture and pour eggs over mix. Stir eggs till scrambled. May top with cheese.

Linda Clark, Hattiesburg, MS (Book 4)

Ham and Bacon Quiche

12 slices bacon, fried crisp and crumbled

2 deep-dish pie shells, baked and cooled

2 cups chopped ham

2 cups chopped broccoli, cooked

4 tablespoons chopped onion

1 pint half-and-half

10 eggs

10 slices Swiss cheese

2 teaspoons salt

2 teaspoons pepper

Crumble equal amounts of bacon into each pie shell. Layer half of the ham and half of the broccoli in each pie shell. Add half the chopped onion to each. In separate bowl, beat together the half-and-half and eggs. Chop Swiss cheese and add to mixture. Add salt and pepper. Pour ½ this mixture over each ham and broccoli quiche. Preheat oven to 500º. Bake for 10 minutes. Reduce heat to 350º and bake for 45 minutes or until knife inserted comes out clean. Can be frozen for later use.

Hannah S. Harris (Book 3)

Kay's Sausage Quiche

1 pound bulk sausage
⅓ cup chopped onion
⅓ cup chopped bell pepper
1½ cups grated sharp Cheddar
  cheese
1 tablespoon flour
1 tablespoon parsley flakes
¾ teaspoon seasoned salt
2 eggs, beaten well
1 cup evaporated milk
¼ teaspoon garlic salt
¼ teaspoon pepper
1 deep-dish pie shell, unbaked

Preheat oven to 375º. In medium skillet, fry sausage until cooked; remove and drain, reserving 2 tablespoons drippings. Sauté onion and bell pepper in drippings for 3 minutes. Combine cheese and flour; stir in cooked sausage, bell pepper, and onion. Mix well. Mix together parsley, seasoned salt, eggs, evaporated milk, garlic salt, and pepper; add to sausage mixture and mix well. Pour into pie shell and bake on cookie sheet for 35–40 minutes or until brown and filling is set. Cool and slice.

Hilda Underwood, Columbus Club (Book 1)

Alexander Graham Bell's experiments proved successful on March 10, 1876, when the first complete sentence was transmitted to his assistant Thomas Watson: "Watson, come here; I want you."

Kenny's Millionaire Gravy

1 pound pork sausage
  (Jimmy Dean)
2–3 tablespoons flour

1 pint half-and-half, divided
Hot biscuits

Fry sausage and remove to another dish, reserving drippings. Stir flour in drippings, then add ½ pint of half-and-half and let simmer to make a white roux. Mix sausage into white roux. Add the remaining ½ pint of half-and-half to give a good consistency; simmer slowly. Gravy will be thick. Pour over hot biscuits.

Gail Voss Lewis, Summit, MS (Book 4)

Tomato Gravy

4 tablespoons bacon drippings
2–3 heaping tablespoons flour
Salt and pepper to taste

1 cup peeled, chopped tomatoes
2–3 cups cold water

Heat bacon drippings in heavy skillet. Add flour, salt and pepper. Stir to mix and continue stirring until evenly browned (medium to dark brown), being careful not to burn. Add tomatoes; stir quickly, and very carefully add water, stirring carefully. Reduce heat to prevent boil-over; stir occasionally while cooking about 30 minutes, or until the mixture cooks to a desired consistency.

Angela L. McCoy, Jackson Council (Book 3)

Ham and Swiss Cheese Sandwiches

2 tablespoons butter or
  margarine, softened
2 teaspoons finely chopped
  onion
2 teaspoons mustard with
  horseradish

¾ teaspoon poppy seeds
  or sesame seeds
2 hamburger buns
2 slices cooked ham
2 slices Swiss cheese

Combine butter, onion, mustard, and poppy or sesame seeds; mix well. Spread on both sides of hamburger buns. Place 1 ham slice and 1 cheese slice on bottom of each bun; cover with top bun. Wrap each sandwich in foil and bake at 350º for 25 minutes. Makes 2 servings.

Eurcle Culipher, Jackson North Council (Book 2)

Soups, Stews, and Chilies

1882
Three-Box

This oak-encased instrument was the standard for many years and one of the first to place the crank more conveniently on the side. The top box contained a ringer and a switchhook. The middle box was a Blake transmitter, which was known for its improved voice clarity. The bottom, a cover for a wet cell battery, doubled as a writing shelf. To place a call, you turned the crank to ring the operator, then picked up the receiver. The operator would then answer and connect you to the party you wished to call. To signal the operator to disconnect the call, you would hang up the receiver and turn the crank to produce a short ring. This was called "ringing off."

Broccoli Soup

Easy to make and delicious.

1 (10-ounce) can chicken broth,
  or 3 bouillon cubes and
  2 cups water
1 (10-ounce) package frozen,
  chopped broccoli

2 tablespoons cornstarch
2 cups milk
¼ pound mild Velveeta
  jalapeño cheese, cubed

Bring chicken broth or bouillon cubes and water to a boil in 2-quart saucepan. Add broccoli; cook over medium heat until just tender. Add cornstarch dissolved in milk, and cheese. Heat and stir until thickened. Do not boil.

Blanche Maxwell, McComb, MS (Book 4)

Broccoli-Cheese Soup

1 (10-ounce) package frozen,
  chopped broccoli
1 (10-ounce) can chicken broth
2 teaspoons chicken bouillon,
  or 2 cubes
2 cups chopped onion
½ cup chopped celery
Pepper to taste

½ cup milk
2 tablespoons butter or
  margarine
2 tablespoons cornstarch with
  enough milk to dissolve
3 cups cubed cheese (2 cups
  Cheddar and 1 cup Velveeta)

Boil first 5 ingredients until barely tender; purée in blender for about 3 seconds. Add pepper and return to medium-low heat. Add milk, butter, and cornstarch mixture. Blend and stir until hot. Add cheese. Heat until cheese melts and soup is thickened, stirring constantly. Do not boil.

Martha Alice Minyard, Tupelo Council (Book 3)

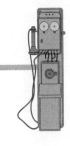

"I Don't Feel Good" Cheese Soup

4 tablespoons butter (do not use margarine)
4 large bunches green onions, finely chopped
4 stalks celery, finely chopped
1 (10¾-ounce) can cream of chicken soup
2 (10-ounce) cans chicken broth
3 cans water
1 package (16 slices) Kraft American cheese singles
Salt to taste

In large stockpot, sauté butter, onions, and celery until very tender. Add remaining ingredients except cheese and salt. Mix well so that soup is not lumpy. Bring to a boil, stirring occasionally. Reduce to medium heat and add unwrapped cheese slices, one at a time, while stirring. Add salt. Continue cooking, uncovered, for 1 hour. Serve with hot buttered crescent rolls or Hawaiian rolls for dipping and sopping.

Peggy Runnels, Mendenhall MS (Book 4)

Creamy Asparagus Soup

1 (16-ounce) can asparagus tips with liquid
¼ cup chopped onion
¼ cup chopped celery
1 cup cooked rice
1½ cups milk
Black pepper to taste
Dash of nutmeg

Place asparagus with liquid, onion, celery, and cooked rice in blender; blend on low speed until puréed. Pour into a saucepan; add milk. Season and heat to boiling point. Serve immediately.

Vickie Folds, Natchez Council (Book 3)

Potato Soup

3 medium potatoes, peeled
  and cubed
1 medium onion, grated
1 large stalk celery, grated
1 (10-ounce) can chicken broth

1¼ cups water
¼ teaspoon white pepper
1 teaspoon dried parsley
1 teaspoon minced green onion

Combine all ingredients, except green onions, in saucepan. Bring to a boil; cover, reduce heat, and simmer for 30 minutes or until potatoes are tender. Remove 1 cup of the soup mixture; process in blender, then return to saucepan; heat thoroughly. Garnish with minced green onions.

Note: If no blender is available, potatoes can be mashed by hand.

Helen Graham, Jackson Council (Book 3)

Potato Soup

10 medium potatoes, peeled
  and diced
1 (10¾-ounce) can cream of
  celery soup
1 (10¾-ounce) can cream of
  onion soup
1 (10¾-ounce) can cream of
  mushroom soup

Salt and pepper to taste
Tabasco to taste
1 pound Velveeta cheese,
  cubed
1 stick margarine
1 (5-ounce) can evaporated milk

Cover diced potatoes with water and boil until tender. Leave potatoes in water. Add the three soups. Add salt, pepper, and Tabasco to taste. In a separate pan, melt cheese and margarine slowly. Add evaporated milk to cheese mixture. Mix all together and enjoy. This makes a large amount.

Irene (Mrs. Jasper) Lipscomb, Macon, MS (Book 4)

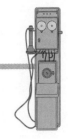

Egg Drop Soup

6 cups chicken broth
2 tablespoons cornstarch,
  dissolved in 2 tablespoons
  water
1 tablespoon soy sauce

½ teaspoon sugar
2 eggs, lightly beaten
Salt and pepper to taste
2 scallions, sliced with green
  tops, for garnish

Bring broth to a boil. Combine cornstarch mixture with soy sauce and sugar. Slowly stir into broth and continue stirring until soup is thickened and clear; remove from heat. Gradually add beaten eggs, stirring with fork until eggs separate in shreds. Season with salt and pepper. Serve immediately garnished with sliced scallions.

Gayle Hall, Tupelo Club, Baldwyn, MS (Book 4)

Fantastic French Onion Soup

3 large onions, thinly sliced
¼ cup butter, melted
3 chicken bouillon cubes, or
  1 tablespoon granules
2 beef bouillon cubes, or
  2 teaspoons granules
5 cups boiling water

½ teaspoon salt
Dash of pepper
½ teaspoon Kitchen Bouquet
French bread, sliced 1 inch thick
  (optional)
Swiss cheese, sliced (optional)

Sauté onion slices in butter over medium-low heat until onions are tender. Dissolve bouillon in boiling water, then add to onions. Add salt, pepper, and Kitchen Bouquet. Bring to a boil, then reduce heat. Simmer, uncovered, for 1 hour.

If desired, put 1 slice French bread in bottom of oven-proof bowl; ladle soup over bread and top with 1 slice Swiss cheese. Place under broiler until cheese melts, about 3–4 minutes.

Donna Graffagnino, Hattiesburg Council (Book 3)

Three Bean Soup

½ pound dried Great
  Northern beans
½ pound dried red kidney
  beans
½ pound pink or pinto beans
Water
2 tablespoons butter or
  margarine

1 medium onion, finely chopped
1½ pounds smoked neck
  bones or ham hocks
1 bay leaf
7 cups water
½ pound smoked sausage
  or kielbasa, sliced
Salt and pepper to taste

Rinse beans; discard any stones. In large stockpot or kettle, heat beans and 8 cups water to boiling. Boil for 2 minutes. Remove from heat; cover and let stand 1 hour. Drain beans in colander and rinse with water.

In same stockpot, heat butter and cook onion until tender, stirring occasionally. Add smoked neck bones or ham hocks, bay leaf, and 7 cups water. Heat to boiling. Add drained beans; return to a boil. Cover and simmer beans about 1 hour or until almost tender, stirring occasionally. Add smoked sausage and cook 15 minutes more or until beans are soft. Remove bay leaf and neck bones or ham hocks. Cool slightly and trim meat from bones; add to soup. Discard bay leaf and bones. Add salt and pepper to taste. Makes about 8 servings.

Sheila Moore (Book 3)

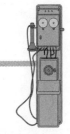

Black Bean Soup

2 tablespoons vegetable oil
1 onion, chopped
1 teaspoon chopped garlic
1 tablespoon cumin
2 teaspoons chili powder
3 (15-ounce) cans black beans,
   divided

3 cups chicken stock, divided
2 tablespoons lime juice
3 cups chunky salsa
1 (4-ounce) can green chiles
Dashes of Louisiana hot sauce
Sour cream, Cheddar cheese,
   and green onions (optional)

Heat oil; add onion, garlic, cumin, and chili powder. Sauté 4 minutes; set aside. Purée 2 cans black beans in 2 batches, adding 1½ cups chicken stock to each. Pour puréed beans into onion mixture and bring to simmer. Add remaining can beans, lime juice, salsa, green chiles, and hot sauce. Simmer 30 minutes. Serve in individual bowls topped with dollop of sour cream, a sprinkling of Cheddar cheese, and green onion, if desired.

Virginia Shaw, Smithdale, MS (Book 4)

Taco Soup

2 pounds ground beef
3 large onions, chopped
1 (10-ounce) can Ro-Tel
   tomatoes
3 (28-ounce) cans stewed
   tomatoes
1 (16-ounce) can kidney or
   pinto beans, undrained

1 (11-ounce) can whole-kernel
   corn, undrained
1 (1-ounce) package dry ranch
   dressing mix
2 teaspoons dry fiesta ranch
   dressing mix

Brown beef and onion. Drain, then place in crockpot with all other ingredients; mix. Cook for 3–4 hours on LOW.

Jewel Boone, McComb, MS; Janet McCoy, Gay Thomas Russell
(Book 4)

Chicken Tortilla Soup

1 pound cooked chicken,
  cubed
1 (14-ounce) can diced
  tomatoes with green pepper
  and onions
1 (15-ounce) can green beans,
  drained
1 (11-ounce) can Mexicorn,
  drained
1 (14-ounce) can chicken broth
1 (4-ounce) can green chiles
1 (1-ounce) package taco
  seasoning mix
8–10 soft corn tortillas, cut
  into strips
4 cups water
1 (8-ounce) package shredded
  mozzarella cheese

Mix all ingredients together in large stockpot, except cheese; bring to a boil. Add mozzarella cheese; serve when cheese melts.

Brandy Duncan, Brandon, MS (Book 4)

Basic Recipe for 5-Can Soup

1 (15-ounce) can Veg-All
1 (11-ounce) can whole-kernel
  corn
1 (15-ounce) can chili (with or
  without beans)
1 (10-ounce) can Ro-Tel
  tomatoes
1 (14½-ounce) can stewed
  tomatoes

Empty all cans into large crockpot; add a little water (as you like). Let your imagination go to work. You may substitute a can of beef stew with vegetables for the chili, or add ground meat, onions, okra, leftovers from the refrigerator, canned chili beans, or red beans—just about anything. I like to start mine early and let it cook for several hours. Of course, you must have a 'pone of cracklin' cornbread to go with it.

Emma Zell Knighton, Centerville, MS (Book 4)

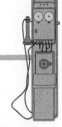

Shake-Rattle-Ro-Tel Soup

2 pounds ground round
2 large onions, chopped
1 (10-ounce) can Ro-Tel
   tomatoes and green chiles
3 (10¾-ounce) cans minestrone
   soup

1 (15-ounce) can lima beans
2 soup cans water
Salt and pepper to taste
1 bay leaf

Brown meat and onions. Drain, if necessary. Add remaining ingredients and cook over low heat 1–1½ hours. Serve with cornbread or French bread. Even better reheated the next day.

Betty Cryder (Book 3)

Corn Chowder

6 bacon strips
3 ribs celery, chopped
2 medium onions, chopped
3 tablespoons minced garlic
3 cups chicken stock
3 medium baking potatoes,
   peeled and diced

3 (11-ounce) cans whole-kernel
   corn
1 (7-ounce) can creamed corn
2 pints half-and-half
Salt and pepper to taste
Pinch of nutmeg

Sauté bacon in medium soup pot, being careful not to burn; remove, cool, and crumble; set aside. In drippings, sauté celery, onions, and garlic until tender. Add stock and potatoes. Cover and simmer 30 minutes over medium heat. Add corn, creamed corn, and half-and-half. Stir well. Cover and cook over low heat 15 minutes. Add crumbled bacon, salt, pepper, and nutmeg. Let rest 15 minutes before serving. If too thin, thicken with cornstarch or flour mixed with stock or cream.

Carolyn Hale, Ellisville, MS (Book 4)

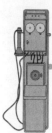

Crabmeat Bisque

2 (10¾-ounce) cans tomato
  soup
1 (10¾-ounce) can green
  pea soup
2 pints half-and-half

1 pound crabmeat
Lea & Perrins Worcestershire
  sauce to taste
Sherry wine to taste

Blend soups and bring almost to a boil. Add half-and-half slowly. Add crabmeat and Worcestershire sauce; simmer for a few minutes. Add sherry to taste and keep warm. This may be served on toast or in a small cup or bowl.

Betty Brockman, Hattiesburg Council (Book 1)

Oyster Soup

1 tablespoon chopped onion
1 tablespoon butter or
  margarine
1½ tablespoons all-purpose
  flour

1½ cups milk
½ teaspoon salt
½ pint oysters, drained
⅓ teaspoon chopped parsley

Sauté onion in butter until tender; add flour, stirring until smooth. Cook 1 minute, stirring constantly. Gradually add milk, and cook over medium heat until thick and bubbly. Stir in salt. In a separate pan, cook oysters over medium low heat until edges start to curl up, about 5 minutes, then add to soup mixture. Sprinkle parsley over soup and serve hot. Yields 2 servings.

Eurcle Culipher, Jackson North Council (Book 2)

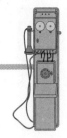

Duck Gumbo

1 cup flour
1½ sticks margarine
2 quarts duck broth
2 ducks, well cooked and
  boned
4 medium onions, finely
  chopped
1 small bunch celery, diced
1 large or 3 small green bell
  peppers, diced
1 bunch green onions (green
  and white), finely chopped

3 cloves garlic
1 (6-ounce) can tomato paste
2 (20-ounce) cans tomatoes
2 teaspoons Ac'cent
2 tablespoons dry parsley flakes
1 teaspoon oregano
1 teaspoon thyme
2 tablespoons salt
1 tablespoon black pepper
2 tablespoons gumbo filé
1 teaspoon red pepper, or to taste

In cast-iron skillet, brown flour in margarine slowly to make roux. Add roux to broth in large stockpot; mix well. Add meat and chopped vegetables to broth mixture and set aside. Combine with remaining ingredients and mix all together in pot; bring to a boil, turn down and simmer 2 hours, stirring often. Serve over hot cooked rice.

Mrs. James T. Cash, Greenwood Council (Book 2)

A practical telephone was actually invented independently by two men working in the United States, Elisha Gray and Scottish-born Alexander Graham Bell. Incredibly, both men filed for a patent on their designs at the New York patent office on February 14, 1876, with Bell beating Gray by only two hours!

Seafood Gumbo

1 cup vegetable oil or bacon
  drippings
1 cup all-purpose flour
2 large onions, chopped
2 stalks celery, chopped
1 large green bell pepper,
  chopped
6 cloves garlic, minced
1 gallon warm water
4 cups sliced okra
3 tomatoes, peeled, chopped

2 tablespoons salt
Red and black pepper to taste
1 pint oysters, undrained
1 pound fresh or frozen
  crabmeat
1½–2 pounds fresh or frozen
  medium shrimp, peeled,
  deveined
½ cup chopped parsley
½ cup chopped green onion tops
Gumbo filé (optional)

Combine oil and flour in an iron pot over medium heat; cook, stirring constantly, until roux is the color of a copper penny, about 10–15 minutes. Add onions, celery, green bell pepper, and garlic to roux; cook, stirring constantly, until vegetables are tender. (Do not let roux burn as it will ruin gumbo; reduce heat, if necessary.) Gradually add warm water to roux, in small amounts at first, blending well after each addition. Add okra and tomatoes. Bring mixture to a boil. Reduce heat; simmer, stirring occasionally, at least 20 minutes (1–1½ hours is better as it develops more flavor at this point). Stir in salt, pepper, and seafood. Bring gumbo to a boil; simmer 10 minutes. Add parsley and green onions; simmer 5 minutes longer. Remove from heat and serve gumbo over hot rice. Gumbo can be further thickened, if desired, by adding a small amount of filé to each serving. Yields 12–14 servings.

Note: Almost any kind of meat, poultry or game can be substituted for seafood products.

Dolores Thomas, Meridian Council (Book 1)

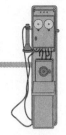

Shrimp Gumbo

2 cups sliced fresh okra, or
   1 (10-ounce) package frozen
   okra, sliced
½ cup oil
1 pound shrimp, fresh or
   frozen, peeled and deveined
⅔ cup chopped green onions
   with tops

3 cloves garlic, finely chopped
Black pepper to taste
2 cups water
1 cup canned tomatoes
2 whole bay leaves
6 drops Tabasco
1½ cups cooked rice

Sauté okra in oil for 10 minutes. Add shrimp, onions, garlic, and pepper. Cook for about 5 minutes. Add water, tomatoes, and bay leaves. Cover and simmer for 20 minutes. Remove the bay leaves and add Tabasco. Place ¼ cup of cooked rice in each of 6 soup bowls. Fill with gumbo and serve.

Bonnie L. Woodward, Natchez Council (Book 3)

Ranch Stew

1 pound ground meat
1 onion, chopped
1 green bell pepper, chopped
1 (14-ounce) can diced tomatoes
1 (8-ounce) can whole-kernel
   corn

1 (16-ounce) can pinto beans
1 tablespoon sugar
Salt to taste
1 tablespoon chili powder
1 pod garlic, diced
Dash of red pepper

Brown ground meat, pepper, and onion in large skillet. Add remaining ingredients and mix well. Cover and simmer for 1 hour.

Betty Staples, Laurel, MS (Book 4)

Irish Stew

4 white onions, sliced
1 (3-pound) shoulder of lamb or beef, cut into 1½-inch cubes
8 carrots, peeled and sliced
8 celery ribs, sliced
Salt and pepper to taste
1½ teaspoons chopped fresh rosemary

½ teaspoon dried rosemary
6 potatoes, cut into ⅓-inch-thick slices
2 cups chicken, veal, or beef stock
2 cups white or red wine
Chopped parsley for garnish

Place a layer of onions into large pot, then add layers of lamb or beef cubes, carrots, and celery. Season each layer with salt, pepper, and rosemary. Repeat layers; finishing with potatoes. Pour in stock and wine; bring stew to a boil. Skim off top, if necessary. Lower heat and cook for 2½–3 hours. Garnish with parsley. Serves 6–8 people.

T. J. Smith, McComb Council (Book 3)

Mississippi Irish Stew

2 pounds cubed meat
½ cup butter or margarine
Salt and pepper to taste
2 large potatoes, peeled and sliced
1 (17-ounce) can whole-kernel corn

1 (17-ounce) can English peas
3 medium carrots, peeled and thinly sliced
1 (4-ounce) can sliced mushrooms
1 large onion, chopped
1 (15-ounce) can tomatoes

Brown beef in butter; season with salt and pepper. Layer vegetables in crockpot, then add browned meat. Cook for 3–4 hours on LOW.

Zula Collins, Greenwood Council (Book 2)

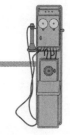

Meatball Stew

1½ pounds ground beef
1 egg, slightly beaten
1 cup bread crumbs
¼ cup chopped onion
1 teaspoon salt
1 (10½-ounce) can condensed
  beef broth

1 (10¾-ounce) can condensed
  tomato soup
¼ teaspoon thyme
1 (16-ounce) can mixed
  vegetables, drained
1 (16-ounce) can whole white
  potatoes, drained

Combine beef, egg, bread crumbs, onion, and salt; mix well. Shape into 50 meatballs. Brown meatballs in a large heavy pan; pour off fat. Add remaining ingredients. Cook over medium heat 30 minutes; stir occasionally. Serves 6.

Susan Easley, Jackson North Council (Book 1)

"My Daddy's" Chili

1½ pounds ground beef
1 large onion, chopped
2 garlic cloves, minced
1 tablespoon butter
1 (8-ounce) can tomato sauce
1 (16-ounce) can tomatoes
1 teaspoon cumin salt

2 tablespoons chili powder
1 tablespoon paprika
1½ teaspoons minced hot
  red pepper
1 (16-ounce) can red beans,
  rinsed, drained (optional)

Sauté ground beef, onion, and garlic in butter. Add other ingredients and cook slowly for 2 hours or longer.

Gay T. Russell, Jackson South Council (Book 2)

Nevada Annie's Champion Chili

3 medium onions, chopped
2 medium bell peppers, seeded
  and chopped
2 large stalks celery, chopped
2 small cloves garlic, minced
½ small fresh jalapeño
  pepper, sliced
8 pounds lean ground beef
1 (4-ounce) can green chiles
2 (14.5-ounce) cans stewed,
  diced tomatoes

1 (15-ounce) can tomato sauce
1 (6-ounce) can tomato paste
2 (3-ounce) bottles chili powder
2 tablespoons cumin
Tabasco to taste
2–3 bay leaves
Garlic salt to taste
Salt and pepper to taste
½ (12-ounce) can beer
1 (12-ounce) bottle mineral
  water

Sauté first 5 ingredients. Add meat and brown. Add remaining ingredients, including ½ can beer (drink the remainder!). Add water just to cover the top. Cook about 3 hours on low heat; stir often. Makes 24 or more servings. Freezes well.

R. W. Dees, Jackson South Council (Book 2)

Salads

1892
Desk Set

The first common battery arrange-
ment came into play in the 1890s,
providing electricity to all telephones
controlled by the central office. Previously,
each customer's telephone needed its own battery to
power the transmitter. The innovation of the common battery changed telephone design. The big, bulky wall sets
with wet batteries providing power and cranks to signal
the operator could now be replaced with sleek desk sets.
Since the crank and batteries were no longer required, the
subset could be mounted on the wall and out of the way.
When you wanted to place a call, you would simply pick
up the receiver and wait for the operator. When you fin-
ished your call, you could just hang up. Long-distance calling reached a major milestone in 1892, when telephone
service between New York and Chicago began. This
950–mile circuit was the longest line possible with the exist-
ing technology.

Chinese Cabbage Slaw

1 tablespoon sugar
⅓ cup apple cider vinegar
1 tablespoon sesame oil

10 cups shredded cabbage
1 tablespoon sesame seeds,
toasted

Combine first 3 ingredients; pour over cabbage and toss gently. Cover and chill for at least 8 hours. Before serving, toss gently and sprinkle with sesame seeds.

Angela L. McCoy, Jackson Council (Book 3)

Cornbread Salad

This is better the next day.

1 pan cornbread, cooled
8 slices bacon, cooked in
   microwave and crumbled
1 medium onion, chopped
2 hard-boiled eggs, chopped
   (optional)

1 green bell pepper, chopped
   (optional)
2 large tomatoes, chopped
1 cup mayonnaise

Crumble cornbread; add bacon and onion. If desired, add eggs and bell pepper. Add tomatoes and mayonnaise last. Stir gently. Chill until served.

Josie Reynolds, Meridian Council (Book 3)

Corn Salad

2 (11-ounce) cans Mexicorn,
  drained
1 green bell pepper, chopped
2 cucumbers, peeled and diced
1 onion, chopped
3 tablespoons mayonnaise
1 tomato, chopped

Combine Mexicorn, bell pepper, cucumbers, onion, and mayonnaise. Cover and chill. Add tomato before serving.

Mrs. F. E. (Peggy) Robertson, Columbus Club (Book 1)

Black-Eyed Pea Salad

½ pound dried black-eyed peas
2 slices bacon, uncooked
1 medium onion
2 cloves garlic
½ teaspoon salt
4 cups water
1 (6-ounce) jar marinated
  artichoke hearts
1 tablespoon Dijon mustard
1 tablespoon Worcestershire
½ pound spinach leaves
4 slices bacon, cooked and
  crumbled

Sort and wash peas; place in a Dutch oven. Add 2 slices uncooked bacon and next 4 ingredients. Bring to a boil; cover, reduce heat, and simmer for 40 minutes or until peas are tender. Drain. Remove and discard bacon, onion, and garlic. Keep peas warm. Drain artichoke hearts, reserving marinade. Chop artichoke hearts and add to black-eyed peas. Combine reserved marinade, mustard, and Worcestershire; pour over peas and toss gently. Arrange spinach leaves on individual salad plates; spoon salad onto spinach. Sprinkle with crumbled bacon and serve warm. Makes 6 servings.

Angela L. McCoy, Jackson Council (Book 3)

Bean Salad

1 (14.5-ounce) can French-style
  green beans
1 (16-ounce) can yellow beans
1 (17-ounce) can Niblet corn
1 (15-ounce) can English peas
1 (3-ounce) jar chopped
  pimentos

1 onion, chopped
1 cup sugar
¾ cup vinegar
½ cup Wesson oil
1 teaspoon salt
½ teaspoon pepper

Drain the beans, corn, peas, and pimentos. Mix together with chopped onion. Bring sugar and vinegar to a boil, then add oil and return to a boil. Add salt and pepper. Pour over vegetables, mix, and refrigerate for 24 hours.

Patricia Bain, Kosciusko Club (Book 2)

Mexican Three-Bean Salad

1 (15-ounce) can pinto beans,
  drained
1 (15-ounce) can green beans,
  drained
1 (15-ounce) can yellow beans,
  drained
½ cup chopped onion

½ cup chopped bell pepper
¼ cup sugar
¼ cup vinegar
¼ cup salad oil
2 tablespoons hot chili sauce
1 teaspoon salt
1 teaspoon black pepper

Place beans, onion, and bell pepper in large container with cover. Combine remaining ingredients, mixing well. Pour over vegetables. Chill in refrigerator at least 4 hours before serving.

J. H. Barner, Tupelo Council (Book 1)

Fiesta Salad

1 medium head lettuce
1 (15-ounce) can Ranch Style
  beans, drained and rinsed
3 cups shredded Cheddar
  cheese
2 tomatoes, diced
1 onion, chopped (optional)

1 (8-ounce) bottle Catalina
  dressing
¾ pound ground chuck,
  browned and drained
1 (10-ounce) package Fritos,
  crushed

Prepare lettuce as usual for salad. Add beans to lettuce. Add shredded cheese, tomatoes, onion, if desired, dressing, and meat; chill. Just before serving, top with Fritos.

Kent Holden and Ida Lee Barron, Jackson North Council (Book 1)

Seven-Layer Lettuce Salad

1 medium head lettuce,
  washed and drained
½ cup chopped green bell
  pepper (also red, if desired)
½ cup chopped onion
½ cup chopped celery
1 can water chestnuts, chopped

1 (10-ounce) package frozen
  peas, thawed
2 cups mayonnaise
2 tablespoons sugar
½ cup shredded Cheddar
  cheese
Bacon bits (optional)

Prepare lettuce as usual for salad. In a large bowl, layer vegetables as listed above. Mix mayonnaise with sugar. Dot over salad and spread carefully over top to sides. Sprinkle cheese on top; add bacon bits, if desired. Make the night before; cover and refrigerate.

Ellen F. Horsman, Jackson South Council (Book 1)

Marvelous Green Salad

1 head lettuce, pinched into
bite-size pieces
1 (7-ounce) can English peas,
drained
¾ cup chopped celery
½ large bell pepper, chopped
1 cup chopped green onions

1½ cups mayonnaise
2 tablespoons sugar
½ (3-ounce) shaker Parmesan
cheese
Bacon bits for garnish

Place about ¾ of the lettuce in a large flat dish or pan. Sprinkle peas over lettuce, then celery, bell pepper, green onions, and remaining lettuce. Cover with mayonnaise. Mix sugar with Parmesan. Sprinkle over mayonnaise. Cover and refrigerate for 1–2 days. Just before serving, sprinkle with bacon bits.

Laura McClelland, Capitol Life Member Club (Book 2)

English Pea Salad

1 (15-ounce) can English peas,
drained
2 hard-boiled eggs, chopped
1 cup chopped onion

2 tablespoons mayonnaise
¼ cup red wine vinegar
Salt and pepper to taste

Combine peas, eggs, and onion with mayonnaise and vinegar; salt and pepper to taste. Toss lightly. Cover and chill until serving.

Jolene Baker, Gulf Coast Council (Book 2)

Spinach Salad
with Honey Dressing

¼ teaspoon salt
1 clove garlic, crushed
⅓ cup honey
⅓ cup light olive oil
1 tablespoon lemon juice
¾ pound fresh spinach,
   rinsed and drained

1 (8-ounce) can Mandarin
   oranges, drained
¾ cup coarsely chopped
   walnuts

Sprinkle salt into salad bowl and rub garlic into salt, using the back of a wooden spoon. Add honey, oil, and lemon juice; beat with a wire whisk. Refrigerate. Add spinach and remaining ingredients to dressing; toss gently. Yields 4–6 servings.

Angela L. McCoy, Jackson Council (Book 3)

Linda's Broccoli Salad

4 cups broccoli florets, cut into
   bite-size pieces
1 cup diced boiled chicken
   breast
½ cup golden raisins

½ cup sliced almonds
½ cup cooked and crumbled
   bacon
½ cup chopped celery
½ cup chopped green onions

Mix salad ingredients together.

DRESSING:
½ cup mayonnaise
½ cup sugar

¼ cup white wine vinegar

Mix Dressing ingredients and toss with salad.

Helen Alexander, Hattiesburg Council (Book 3)

Marinated Greek Salad

This salad is very good with any kind of meat.

2 cups chopped cauliflower
2 cups chopped broccoli
1 cup sliced fresh mushrooms
¾ cup pitted ripe black olives
¾ cup green salad olives

12 cherry tomatoes
1 (8-ounce) bottle Italian
   dressing
4 ounces feta cheese, crumbled

Combine all ingredients, except cheese; refrigerate overnight. Just before serving, add crumbled feta cheese. Serves 6–8.

Mary W. Bryant, Capitol Life Member (Book 2)

Cauliflower Salad

1 head cauliflower
½ (10-ounce) jar salad olives,
   chopped
3 tomatoes, peeled and
   chopped

1 cup chopped green onions
½ (4.4-ounce) jar Bac-Os
½ pound Cheddar cheese,
   grated
½ cup mayonnaise

Break cauliflower into small pieces; mix well with olives, tomatoes, and onions. Add Bac-Os and grated cheese. Mix mayonnaise with this and let sit for 2–3 hours in refrigerator before serving.

Flora G. "Rosie" Permenter (Book 3)

Artichoke Salad

1 (10.7-ounce) box chicken-
flavor Rice-A-Roni
1 (6-ounce) jar marinated
artichoke hearts, drained,
diced
3 green onions, chopped
1 (10-ounce) jar sliced green
olives, drained
2–3 tablespoons mayonnaise

Cook Rice-A-Roni as directed on package; let cool. Mix in artichoke hearts, green onions, and olives. Stir in mayonnaise and refrigerate until served.

Betty Staples, Laurel, MS (Book 4)

Artichoke Rice Salad

1 package fried rice and
vermicelli with almonds
(Rice-A-Roni)
2 tablespoons butter
4 green onions, chopped
1 bell pepper, chopped
1 (14-ounce) can chicken broth
1 (8-ounce) can sliced water
chestnuts, drained, chopped
1 (4-ounce) can sliced black
olives, drained
1 (12-ounce) can white chicken
breast, drained
1 cup mayonnaise
1 small can artichokes, drained,
chopped

Brown rice in butter until vermicelli is golden. Add onions and pepper and sauté until tender. Add broth and seasoning packet from rice. Cook about 15 minutes or as directions indicate on the box. Cool. Add remaining ingredients. Store in refrigerator until ready to serve.

Hope Conerly, Jackson, MS (Book 4)

Sour Cream Cucumbers

½ teaspoon salt
1 tablespoon sugar
1 tablespoon vinegar
1 cup sour cream

2 tablespoons chopped chives
2 tablespoons dill weed
1 teaspoon celery seed
2 firm cucumbers, peeled

Dissolve salt and sugar in vinegar; add sour cream and stir until smooth. Add chives, dill weed, and celery seed. Slice cucumbers paper thin. Combine with dressing and chill at least one hour before serving.

Beth Harbour, Meridian Council (Book2)

Swedish Potato Salad

2 tart apples, cored and thinly
    sliced
2 potatoes, cooked, peeled, and
    thinly sliced
4 sweet gherkin pickles, sliced
1 (3½-ounce) jar herring
    fillets or white albacore tuna,
    drained
1 tablespoon minced or dried
    onion

1 tablespoon minced parsley
½ cup cooking oil, divided
1 hard-boiled egg yolk
½ teaspoon salt
Black pepper to taste
2 tablespoons vinegar
Lettuce
1 (14.5-ounce) can whole beets,
    drained, divided

Combine apples, potatoes, pickles, herring or tuna, onion, and parsley; toss with 1 tablespoon oil. Mash egg yolk; add salt and pepper. Beat in remaining oil until smooth; add vinegar. Add ½ of the sauce to potato mixture with 2 finely minced beets. Arrange salad on lettuce; garnish with remaining whole beets. Pass remaining sauce. Yields 8 servings.

Doris P. Kelly, Jackson North Council (Book 2)

Sour Cream Potato Salad

4 hard-boiled eggs
⅔ cup mayonnaise
¾ cup sour cream
1½ teaspoons prepared
   mustard with horseradish
½ pound bacon

⅓ cup chopped green onions
7 cups cooked and cubed
   potatoes
⅓ cup Italian salad dressing
Salt to taste
Celery seed to taste

Halve eggs and remove yolks. Mash yolks and blend with mayonnaise, sour cream, and mustard. Cook bacon crisp; drain well and crumble. Chop egg whites and combine with bacon, green onions, potatoes, and salad dressing. Fold in mayonnaise mixture and season with salt and celery seed.

Mrs. Ed Collins, Tupelo Council (Book 2)

Cajun Potato Salad

5 pounds small red potatoes,
   unpeeled, halved
1 small bottle liquid crab boil
1–2 cups mayonnaise
1 bunch green onions, chopped
1 pound bacon

2–3 tablespoons red wine
   vinegar
2 teaspoons dry mustard
Few shakes Tony Chachere's
   seasoning

Put potatoes in water and add crab boil when water begins to boil. Drain potatoes when done and let cool.

Meanwhile, cook bacon in oven so it doesn't get too crispy. After potatoes are cool, add remaining ingredients, crumble in bacon, and mix all together. Adjust ingredients to your taste.

Melodye Luke, Gulfport, MS (Book 4)

Sharon's Potato Salad with Shrimp

4 large potatoes, cooked and
diced or thinly sliced, divided

2 tablespoons vegetable oil,
divided

2 tablespoons cider vinegar,
divided

1 teaspoon salt, divided

1 (7-ounce) can shrimp, or fresh,
cleaned and deveined

Dash of onion salt

MSG (optional)

2 heaping tablespoons
mayonnaise

Place half the potatoes in a large bowl; add half the oil, vinegar, and salt. Make another layer of potatoes, oil, vinegar, and salt. Cover and chill overnight.

Before serving, add shrimp, onion salt, MSG, if desired, and mayonnaise; mix well.

Lula Cade, Capitol Life Member (Book 2)

Shrimp Salad

1 (8-ounce) package elbow
macaroni, cooked, drained

2 cups cooked shrimp

1 tablespoon seasoned salt

4 green onions, chopped

1 cup mayonnaise

2 tablespoons parsley flakes

½ teaspoon dill weed

2 hard-boiled eggs, diced

Lettuce

Combine all ingredients, except lettuce, mixing well. Chill 1 hour. Serve on crisp lettuce.

Jeanette Boyd, Gulf Coast Council (Book 2)

Shrimp Mold

1 (10-ounce) can tomato soup, undiluted
1½ tablespoons unflavored gelatin
¼ cup boiling water
1 (8-ounce) package cream cheese, softened
1 pound small shrimp, cooked, peeled, deveined
1 cup mayonnaise
1 cup chopped celery
1 cup chopped green onions
Salt and pepper to taste

Heat soup, undiluted, and let cool. Melt gelatin in boiling water. Mix all ingredients together and pour into greased mold. When set, unmold and serve on lettuce leaves. Beautiful.

Don Gueniot, Jackson South Council (Book 1)

Hot Chicken Salad

4 chicken breasts, boiled and chopped
¾ cup rice, cooked in chicken broth
3 hard-boiled eggs, chopped
½ cup mayonnaise
1 (10¾-ounce) can cream of chicken soup
1 cup chopped celery
1 cup chopped onion
1 (8-ounce) can water chestnuts, drained, chopped
Salt and pepper to taste
1½ cups crushed potato chips, divided

Mix all ingredients, reserving 1 cup crushed potato chips for top. Pour into greased 9x13x2-inch casserole dish. Sprinkle top with reserved potato chips. Bake at 350º for 30 minutes or until hot and bubbly.

Beth Harbour, Meridian, MS (Book 4)

Mill Street Deli Chicken Salad

½ cup mayonnaise
½ cup sour cream
½ teaspoon salt
2 cups cooked and diced
  chicken
1½ cups chopped celery

2 cups chopped hard-boiled
  eggs
½ cup chopped grapes
½ cup slivered almonds
1 teaspoon lemon juice

Mix mayonnaise, sour cream, and salt. Add remaining ingredients. Toss gently. Refrigerate and serve.

Dot Trinkner (Book 3)

Italian Pasta Salmon Salad

2 cups medium shell macaroni
4 radishes, sliced
½ bell pepper, coarsely
  chopped
2 green onions, thinly sliced
¼ cup shredded carrots
3 tablespoons white wine
  vinegar

⅓ cup olive oil
1 clove garlic, minced
½ teaspoon basil
¼ teaspoon dry mustard
1 cup cherry tomatoes, halved
2 (6.5-ounce) cans pink salmon,
  drained, bones removed

Prepare macaroni according to package directions. Drain and cool. Place in large bowl; add radishes, bell pepper, onions, and carrots. In small bowl, combine vinegar, oil, garlic, basil, and mustard. Pour over pasta and vegetables. Toss well; refrigerate for 1–2 hours or overnight. Just before serving, add tomatoes and salmon. Toss gently. Makes 6 (1-cup) servings.

Nella Duckworth (Book 3)

Mediterranean Pasta Salad

DRESSING:

⅔ cup olive oil
½ cup chopped fresh basil
2 tablespoons grated Parmesan
  cheese
¼ teaspoon black pepper

Salt to taste
¼ teaspoon oregano
3 tablespoons red wine vinegar
2 tablespoons chopped green
  onion

Process all Dressing ingredients in a blender until smooth.

SALAD:

1 (12-ounce) package rotelle
  pasta
1 each: yellow, red, and green
  bell pepper, cut in strips
2 fresh tomatoes, cut in wedges

1 (6-ounce) can sliced black
  olives
Feta and/or mozzarella cheese
  (optional)

Cook pasta according to package directions and drain. Put pasta, pepper strips, tomatoes, and olives in a large bowl and pour in Dressing; toss to mix. Add feta cheese and some mozzarella, if desired. Best if served at room temperature.

Hope Conerly, Jackson, MS (Book 4)

In 1877, Bell Telephone Company was formed to operate local telephone exchange operation, installing the first city exchange in Hartford, Connecticut.

Fruit Salad
with Apricot Dressing

APRICOT DRESSING:

1 cup sugar
2 (5½-ounce) cans apricot
  nectar

1 tablespoon cornstarch
1 teaspoon vanilla extract

In saucepan, combine sugar, apricot nectar, and cornstarch until smooth. Cook over medium heat until slightly thickened, stirring often so not to burn or scorch. Stir in vanilla. Cook until thickened a bit more. Remove from heat; cool, then refrigerate.

FRUIT SALAD:

6 large red apples, coarsely
  chopped
8 medium firm bananas, sliced
1 medium fresh pineapple,
  cut into chunks

1 quart fresh strawberries,
  washed, drained, quartered
3–4 kiwi, peeled and sliced
2 cups green seedless grapes,
  halved

In large bowl, combine all fruit. Drizzle with Apricot Dressing. Gently toss to coat. Cover and refrigerate until serving. Yields 26 (1-cup) servings.

Barbara S. Ellis, Canton MS (Book 4)

Waldorf Salad

3 medium-size Red Delicious
  apples, unpeeled, diced
½ cup chopped celery
½ cup seedless red or green
  grapes, halved
½ cup chopped walnuts
¼ cup mayonnaise or salad
  dressing

1½ teaspoons sugar
½ teaspoon lemon juice
¼ cup whipping cream,
  whipped
Nutmeg for garnish

Combine first 4 ingredients in a medium bowl; set aside. Combine mayonnaise, sugar, and lemon juice. Fold in whipped cream and pour over fruit mixture, stirring gently. Sprinkle with nutmeg. Makes 6 servings.

Angela L. McCoy, Jackson Council (Book 3)

Grape Salad

1 (8-ounce) package cream
  cheese, softened
½ cup confectioners' sugar
½ teaspoon vanilla flavoring
1 (8-ounce) container sour cream

2½–3 pounds seedless grapes,
  whole, stemmed
½ cup brown sugar
½ cup chopped pecans

Mix cream cheese, confectioners' sugar, and vanilla in mixer until smooth. Fold in sour cream. Add to washed, drained grapes. Spoon mixture into a 9x13-inch pan. Lightly mix brown sugar and nuts. Sprinkle over grape mixture. Refrigerate a few hours before serving. Do not freeze.

Margie Sasser, Edwards, MS (Book 4)

Orange Cream Fruit Salad

1 (20-ounce) can pineapple
  tidbits, drained
1 (16-ounce) can peach slices,
  drained
1 (11-ounce) can Mandarin
  orange sections, drained
3 medium bananas, sliced
2 medium apples, diced

1 (3-ounce) package vanilla
  instant pudding
1½ cups milk
½ (6-ounce) can frozen orange
  juice concentrate, thawed
  (or ⅓ cup)
¾ cup sour cream

In large bowl, combine fruits; set aside. In small bowl, combine dry pudding mix, milk, and orange juice. Beat with rotary beater till blended (1–2 minutes). Beat in sour cream; fold into fruit mixture. Cover and chill.

Kathy Wilder, Jackson, MS (Book 4)

Hot Pineapple Salad

1 (20-ounce) can pineapple
  chunks, drained, reserve juice
1½ teaspoons cornstarch
¼ cup sugar, brown or white

¼ teaspoon salt
⅓ cup Ritz Cracker crumbs
1½ tablespoons margarine,
  melted

In a saucepan, mix reserved pineapple juice and cornstarch until thoroughly combined. Add sugar and salt; mix thoroughly. Cook over medium heat until clear. Place pineapple in a mixing bowl and add cooked liquid; mix well. Pour mixture into a buttered 8-inch square baking dish. Combine cracker crumbs and melted margarine. Place buttered crumbs over the pineapple mixture. Bake at 350º for 30–40 minutes or until bubbly. Serve hot. Yields 4–6 servings.

Blanche Maxwell, McComb, MS (Book 4)

Melon Ball Salad

1 watermelon, balled, rind
  reserved
2 large cantaloupes, balled
2 cartons small strawberries,
  cleaned, whole
6–8 bananas, sliced

2 (20-ounce) cans pineapple
  chunks, drained
3 (11-ounce) cans Mandarin
  oranges, drained
2 cups seedless grapes

Prepare fruit and put in container with lid on it.

CELERY SEED DRESSING:

1 cup sugar
2 teaspoons dry mustard
2 teaspoons paprika
2 teaspoons celery seed
½ teaspoon salt

1 cup honey
l teaspoon grated lemon or
  lime rind
⅔ cup lemon or lime juice

Mix dressing ingredients, and pour over fruit. Close lid, and put in refrigerator overnight to marinate. This makes enough to fill 2 halves of 1 large watermelon. Serve cold.

Frankie Miller, Greenwood Life Member Club (Book 1)

Strawberry Pretzel Salad

BOTTOM LAYER:

2⅔ cups crushed pretzels   1½ sticks margarine, melted
3 tablespoons sugar

Mix crushed pretzels, sugar, and margarine. Spread in a 9x13 inch pan. Bake at 350º for 10 minutes; cool.

MIDDLE LAYER:

1 (8-ounce) package cream   1 (8-ounce) tub frozen whipped
   cheese, softened   topping, thawed
1 cup sugar

Beat together cream cheese and sugar. Fold in whipped topping. Spread over cooled Bottom Layer.

TOP LAYER:

1 (6-ounce) package strawberry   1 quart frozen strawberries,
   gelatin   unthawed
2 cups boiling water

Mix strawberry gelatin in boiling water. Add frozen strawberries and stir until thawed. Frozen berries will cause the gelatin to set. Pour over Middle Layer. Chill.

Mary P. Cruse, Greenwood Council (Book 3)

Cranberry Salad

1 (6-ounce) or 2 (3-ounce)
  packages cherry-flavored
  Jell-O
2 cups boiling water
1 (6-ounce) can frozen orange
  juice, thawed

1 (7-ounce) can crushed
  pineapple, drained, reserve
  juice
1 (16-ounce) can whole
  cranberry sauce, drained
1 cup chopped nuts

Dissolve Jell-O in boiling water; add orange juice and juice from pineapple with enough water to make 1½ cups liquid. Let stand in refrigerator until it begins to gel. Add cranberry sauce, pineapple, and nuts. Mix and pour into mold and chill.

Liz Matthews, Columbus Club (Book 1)

Coca-Cola Salad

2 (3-ounce) packages cherry-
  flavored Jell-O
2 cups boiling water
1 (16.5-ounce) can black
  cherries, drained, chopped,
  reserve juice

2 (12-ounce) cans Coca-Cola
2 (3-ounce) packages cream
  cheese, softened
1 cup chopped celery
1 cup chopped apples
½ cup chopped nuts (optional)

Dissolve Jell-O in boiling water. Add cherry juice and chopped cherries; add cola. Add cream cheese and stir while hot. Let gel about half way; add remaining ingredients.

Mattie McMinn, Gulf Coast Council and Helen McMullen,
Meridian Council (Book 1)

Kum-Back-Sauce

Delicious on tossed salads, shrimp, and meats.

1 cup Crisco oil
1 tablespoon water
2 medium onions, grated
1 cup tomato ketchup
1 cup chili sauce
2 teaspoons black pepper
2 teaspoons prepared mustard

2 dashes Tabasco
4 garlic cloves, grated
2 cups Kraft Miracle Whip
  salad dressing
2 teaspoons Worcestershire
2 teaspoons paprika
Juice of 2 lemons

Mix all ingredients well. This recipe makes a little over 3 pints. Keeps in refrigerator, and is good as long as it lasts.

Elizabeth Dodds, Jackson North Council (Book 1)

Vegetables

1919
Candlestick

The first dial telephone exchange is credited to Almon B. Strowger who introduced it in LaPorte, Indiana, in 1892. However, it was many years before switching equipment was sufficiently developed to permit dial installation in larger cities. The advent of the vacuum tube amplifier (or repeater) made lines of any length feasible. With repeaters in the line, transcontinental telephone service opened in 1915. Dial service was coming in strongly, and customers could now dial out themselves, with no need to go through an operator. The first dial phones were candlestick phones. To place a call, you lifted the receiver, waited for dial tone, then dialed. The dial tone was a much lower pitched tone than what we hear today. If the switching equipment was busy, dial tone might take several seconds to come on.

Harvard Beets

¾ cup sugar
2 teaspoons cornstarch
⅓ cup water
⅓ cup vinegar
4 cups cooked, sliced beets

3 tablespoons butter or
   margarine
¼ teaspoon salt
¼ teaspoon pepper

Combine sugar, cornstarch, water, and vinegar in saucepan; boil 5 minutes. Add beets and simmer for 30 minutes. Remove from heat; add butter, salt, and pepper. Serves 6.

Edna McKinzie, retired SCB employee, Pioneer Member (Book 3)

Baked Beans

1 pound ground chuck
1 onion, chopped
1 green bell pepper, chopped
3 tablespoons brown sugar

3 tablespoons Worcestershire
½ (14-ounce) bottle ketchup
2 (15-ounce) cans pork and
   beans

Brown meat, onion, and bell pepper, then drain; add sugar, Worcestershire, ketchup, and beans. Bake at 325º in greased casserole for about 45 minutes.

J. T. "Sleepy" Grimes, Jackson North Council (Book 1)

An exchange is a practical means of communicating between many people who have telephones. The first known exchange linking two major cities was established between New York and Boston in 1883.

String Bean Casserole

1 (6-ounce) box fried rice with almonds
1 medium onion, chopped
1 cup mayonnaise
1 (10¾-ounce) can cream soup (celery, mushroom, or chicken)
2 (14.5-ounce) cans French-style green beans
4 cups cooked, diced chicken
1 cup shredded Cheddar cheese
3 slices bread, toasted, buttered, and crumbled

Cook rice according to package directions. Sauté onion and combine with rice. Mix in mayonnaise and soup. Add green beans, chicken, and cheese. Put in greased baking dish, and sprinkle with toasted bread crumbs. Bake 35–40 minutes at 325º.

Verna Deville, McComb Life Club; Georgia Caldwell, Laurel Club;
Mrs. W. G. Morgan, Greenwood Council (Book 1)

Green Bean Casserole

SAUCE:

1¼ cups mayonnaise
1 onion, grated to pulp, with juice
1 teaspoon dry mustard
1 teaspoon Worcestershire
1 teaspoon salt
1 cup grated sharp Cheddar cheese

Mix Sauce ingredients well.

2 (16-ounce) cans whole Blue Lake green beans, drained
1 (8-ounce) can sliced water chestnuts, drained

Layer beans and chestnuts in buttered casserole dish; top with Sauce. Bake at 350º until brown and bubbly. Serves 8.

Susie Douglas, Jackson North Council (Book 2)

Broccoli Casserole

1 large onion, chopped
1 stalk celery, chopped
½ cup mushrooms
2 tablespoons butter
2 (10¾-ounce) cans cream of
  mushroom soup

1 (8-ounce) jar Cheez Whiz
1 cup cooked rice
1 (10-ounce) box frozen,
  chopped broccoli, cooked
  and drained

Sauté onion, celery, and mushrooms in butter. Add soup, Cheez Whiz, rice, and broccoli. Place in casserole dish and cook at 350º for 10–15 minutes.

Sheila Hall, Jackson South Council; Elise Mose, Jackson South Council; Maudie Mosley, Jackson South Council; Mrs. H. B. Walker, Natchez Council; Karyl Duett, Meridian Council; Liz Matthews, Columbus Club; Vivian Holliday, Columbus Club; Joan Franklin, Jackson North Council; Debbie Sellers, Greenwood Council; Cindy Necaise, Gulf Coast Council; Margaretta Pounders, Columbus Club; Etta Tawan, Jackson North Council (Book 1)

Corn Casserole

2 (15-ounce) cans creamed corn
2 eggs, well beaten
6 tablespoons oil

1 teaspoon garlic powder
¾ cup self-rising cornmeal
1 cup grated Cheddar cheese

Grease and flour a 9x13x2-inch baking dish. Mix all ingredients together except cheese. Pour ½ corn mixture in dish; cover with cheese. Top with remaining corn mixture. Bake at 350º for 30–45 minutes.

Frances Welch (Book 3)

Mexicorn Casserole

1 onion, chopped
1 pound ground chuck
Salt and pepper to taste
1 can Van Camp's Spanish rice
1 (8-ounce) can tomato sauce

1 (7-ounce) or (11-ounce) can
  Mexicorn
½ teaspoon chili powder
Grated Cheddar cheese

In large skillet (or electric skillet), brown onion and ground chuck; drain if desired; salt and pepper to taste. Add Spanish rice, tomato sauce, Mexicorn, and chili powder. Mix together and cook over medium heat for 20–25 minutes, stirring occasionally. Spoon cheese over top of mixture and cook until cheese is melted.

Margie Sasser, Edwards, MS (Book 3)

Old-Fashioned Corn Pudding

2 cups corn (fresh is better)
2 cups milk
1 tablespoon sugar
1 teaspoon salt

1 teaspoon nutmeg (optional)
1 stick butter
6 eggs, separated

Mix all ingredients together except egg whites; beat egg whites separately, and fold into corn mixture. Bake until brown in 300°oven. May be made in advance.

Wilma Fenn, McComb Life Club; Geraldine Lyons, Greenwood Council; Jerry Tate, Columbus Club; Elsie Martin, McComb Club (Book 1)

Hominy Casserole

2 (15-ounce) cans hominy,
 drained
1 (4-ounce) can green chile
 peppers, drained
1½ (8-ounce) cartons sour
 cream
1 (8-ounce) package grated
 Monterey Jack cheese

⅓ cup finely chopped onion
1 jalapeño pepper, chopped,
 or to taste
¼ cup fine bread crumbs
¼ cup margarine
Pimento strips

Combine first 6 ingredients in a large bowl. Spoon into 2½-quart greased casserole. Sprinkle with bread crumbs and dot with margarine. Garnish with pimento strips. Bake in 350º oven until bubbly.

Dorothy Thomas, Laurel, MS (Book 4)

Pizza Potatoes

1 box scalloped potatoes
1 (16-ounce) can tomatoes
1½ cups water
½ teaspoon oregano

1 (4-ounce) package sliced
 pepperoni
1 (4-ounce) package shredded
 mozzarella cheese

Empty potatoes and packet of seasoned sauce mix into greased 2-quart casserole dish. Heat tomatoes, water, and oregano until boiling; stir into potatoes. Arrange pepperoni on top and sprinkle with cheese. Bake uncovered at 400° for 30–35 minutes.

Variations: Add or substitute browned and drained ground beef or sausage for pepperoni.

Martha Alice Minyard, Tupelo Council (Book 3)

Potato Dumplings

12 servings instant potatoes
2 eggs, beaten
½ cup plain flour

1 pound bacon, chopped
1 large onion, chopped

Prepare instant potatoes according to package instructions, using a little less water. Let potatoes cool; add eggs and flour; mix well. Form into balls; add to large pan of boiling, salted water and cook for 10 minutes; drain. Fry chopped bacon with onion until crisp; do not drain. Serve over potatoes.

Rita Johnson, Gulf Coast Council (Book 1)

Potato Casserole

2 pounds frozen hash brown
   potatoes, thawed
½ cup margarine, melted
1 teaspoon salt
½ teaspoon pepper
1 pint sour cream

2 (10¾-ounce) cans cream of
   chicken soup
½ cup finely chopped onion
2½ cups shredded Cheddar
   cheese

Combine all ingredients and place in large casserole dish.

TOPPING:
2 cups crushed cornflakes   ½ cup margarine, melted

Mix together and sprinkle on top of casserole. Bake 1–1½ hours at 350º.

*Inez Chustz, Capitol Life Member Club; Anna B. Jackson, Capitol
   Life Member Club; Rubye Nash, Corinth Club; Karyl Duett,
Meridian Council; Susan Goodson, Jackson South Council; Pauline
Heflin, Tupelo Council; Delphine Thornton, Jackson South Council;
   Melissa Smith, Meridian Council; Roma Norman, McComb Club
(Book 1)*

Bob's Cajun Potatoes

1 (5-pound) bag red potatoes
1 stick butter
1 package Lipton Onion Soup
  mix
1/3 cup water

1 tablespoon Tony Chachere's
  Cajun seasoning
2–3 cups shredded sharp
  Cheddar cheese

Cut up enough unpeeled potatoes to fill a 9x13-inch baking dish. In saucepan, melt butter and stir in Lipton onion soup mix, water, and Tony Chachere's seasoning. Pour over potatoes. Bake, covered, 45 minutes at 400° (or 1 hour at 350°). Uncover and sprinkle with Cheddar cheese. Reheat until cheese melts.

Anne Mitchell, Oxford, MS (Book 4)

Sweet Potato Casserole

3 cups cooked, mashed sweet
  potatoes
3/4 cup sugar
1/3 cup milk

1/2 cup butter, softened
1 teaspoon vanilla extract
1 teaspoon salt

Mix all ingredients. Put in buttered casserole dish.

TOPPING:
1/2 cup butter, softened
1/3 cup flour

1 cup brown sugar
1/2 cup chopped nuts

Combine Topping ingredients and sprinkle on top of casserole. Bake at 350º for 30 minutes.

Hazel Walters, Natchez Council; Jean Watkins, Jackson South Council; Jessie Rollins, Capitol Life Member Club; Christine Gaskin, Laurel Club; Rosa Roberts, Greenwood Council; Shirley Guy, Greenwood Council (Book 1)

Bourbon Yams

1 (29-ounce) can whole sweet
   potatoes, drained and cut
   into ½-inch slices
3 tablespoons butter or
   margarine, melted
3 tablespoons brown sugar
3 tablespoons orange juice

3 tablespoons bourbon
¼ teaspoon ground cinnamon
⅛ teaspoon ground cloves
⅛ teaspoon ground nutmeg
½ cup chopped and toasted
   pecans

Place sliced potatoes in lightly greased 8-inch square baking dish. Combine butter and remaining ingredients, except pecans; pour over potatoes. Top with pecans. Bake at 350º for 30 minutes or until thoroughly heated. Yields 4 servings.

Angela L. McCoy, Jackson Council (Book 3)

Onion Pie

5 large yellow onions, chopped
Salt and pepper to taste
¾ stick butter
1 (¼-pound) package crackers,
   crushed

10 slices thin bacon
¾ pound natural Swiss cheese
3 eggs
1 cup sour cream
Paprika

Slice onions, then add salt and pepper, and sauté in butter until tender. Cover bottom of casserole dish with cracker crumbs. Broil bacon until crispy. When onions are very tender, place on top of cracker crumbs along with the butter they were sautéed in. Crumble bacon on top of this. Grate Swiss cheese and sprinkle on top of bacon. Beat the eggs well; add the sour cream and blend well. Pour this mixture over top of cheese. Sprinkle top with paprika. Cover top of casserole dish with foil and bake at 350° for about 35 minutes or until set.

Jane Van Norman, Jackson North Council (Book 1)

Vegetable Casserole

1 (10-ounce) can asparagus,
   drained and cut
1 (15-ounce) can English peas,
   drained
1 hard-boiled egg, chopped

1 (10¾-ounce) can cream of
   mushroom soup
1 cup crushed Ritz Crackers
1 cup grated Cheddar cheese

Mix all ingredients except cheese. Place in a buttered casserole dish and sprinkle cheese on top; bake at 350º for 20 minutes.

Sandy Harrell, Jackson North Council (Book 1)

Asparagus Casserole

1 (10¾-ounce) can cream of
   mushroom soup
1 (15-ounce) can asparagus,
   drained (reserve liquid)
4 hard-boiled eggs, sliced
1 cup grated Cheddar cheese

1 cup cracker crumbs
2 tablespoons margarine,
   divided
2 tablespoons chopped pimiento
1 tablespoon grated onion
   (optional)

Thin soup with asparagus liquid; set aside. In lightly greased casserole dish, make 2 layers of asparagus, sliced eggs, cheese, and cracker crumbs. Dot each layer with margarine and sprinkle with pimiento and onion, if desired. Pour soup mixture over, then bake at 400° for 15 minutes or until bubbly.

Brenda Young, Jackson South Council (Book 2)

Squash Casserole

2 cups chopped fresh squash
1 medium onion, chopped
2 eggs
½ cup milk

1 cup grated cheese
¼ cup margarine, melted
1 sleeve Ritz Crackers, crumbled

Cook squash and onion in salted water to barely cover until tender; drain off all liquid and mash. Beat together eggs and milk; add to squash. Mix cheese, margarine, and cracker crumbs. Add ½ cheese mixture to squash mixture. Pour into buttered casserole dish. Sprinkle remaining crumbs on top. Bake 20–30 minutes at 400º.

Floyce Stanton, Greenwood Council (Book 1)

Squash Casserole

1½ pounds squash
1 stick margarine
1 (8-ounce) package Pepperidge Farm cornbread crumbs

½ cup chopped onion
1 (10¾-ounce) can cream of chicken soup
½ pint sour cream

Cook squash in small amount of salted water until tender; drain. Melt margarine in 2-quart casserole. Stir in crumbs until margarine is absorbed. Remove about ½ the crumbs. Pour squash into casserole; sprinkle with chopped onion. Mix soup with sour cream and spread over vegetables. Sprinkle remaining crumbs on top. Bake at 350º for about 20 minutes or until bubbly.

Mrs. R. T. Alliston, Capitol Life Member Club (Book 2)

Spinach Casserole

4 (10-ounce) packages frozen, chopped spinach
1 medium onion, chopped
1 stick butter
1 (14-ounce) can artichoke hearts, drained, chopped

Celery seed to taste
1 (8-ounce) carton sour cream
Parmesan cheese
Paprika to taste

Cook spinach according to package directions; drain. Sauté onion in butter. Mix spinach, onions, artichoke hearts, celery seed, and sour cream. Top with Parmesan cheese and paprika. Cook in 325º oven until heated thoroughly, about 30 minutes.

Note: Bread crumbs may be added on top.

Mrs. L. N. "Scotty" Palmer, Jackson North Council (Book 1)

Peach Glazed Carrots

1 pound carrots, peeled and sliced
1 cup water

⅓ cup peach preserves
1 tablespoon butter or margarine, melted

Cook carrots in 1 cup boiling water for 5 minutes or until crisp-tender; drain. Combine peach preserves and melted butter; stir into drained carrots. Cook over very low heat until carrots and glaze are thoroughly heated. Yields 4 servings.

Angela L. McCoy, Jackson Council (Book 3)

Eggplant Parmesan

1 large eggplant, peeled and
  sliced
1 egg, beaten
1 cup Italian bread crumbs
Vegetable oil for frying
1 (15-ounce) jar spaghetti sauce

1 (8-ounce) package shredded
  mozzarella cheese
1 (8-ounce) package shredded
  Cheddar cheese
1 cup grated Parmesan cheese

Dip eggplant slices in egg. Coat with bread crumbs. Cook in oil in skillet until brown on both sides. In a 9x13-inch baking dish, alternate layers of spaghetti sauce, eggplant, mozzarella, and Cheddar until all ingredients are used. Top with Parmesan. Bake at 350º until bubbly.

Barbara Staples, Laurel, MS (Book 4)

Eggplant Casserole

1 (16-ounce) can tomatoes
½ teaspoon sugar
2 small garlic cloves, finely
  chopped

2 medium eggplants
Parmesan cheese

Cook tomatoes, sugar, and garlic, covered, while preparing eggplant. Peel and slice eggplant; fry in cooking oil until slightly browned and tender; drain well on paper towels. Place layer of eggplant in casserole dish; spoon part of tomato mixture over eggplant; sprinkle with Parmesan cheese. Continue layering until all ingredients are used. Top with Parmesan cheese. Bake at 350º for about 20 minutes.

Note: Recipe can be easily doubled.

Betty Wier, Greenwood Council (Book 2)

Cabbage Deluxe

4 carrots, each cut in 3 pieces
1 head cabbage, quartered
6–8 small potatoes, halved
2–3 onions (small), chopped

½–1 stick margarine
Salt and pepper to taste
1 cup water

Lay carrots in bottom of Dutch oven. Place cabbage over carrots. Place potatoes and onions around cabbage. Chop margarine and add to vegetables. Add salt, pepper, and water. Bring to a slight boil. Cover and simmer for 1 hour. Do not stir. Serve with cornbread.

Carolyn C. Keyes, Laurel, MS (Book 4)

Stuffed Peppers

½ cup rice
3 large green bell peppers
1¼ pounds ground beef
1 onion, chopped
Salt and pepper to taste

2 (8-ounce) cans tomato sauce,
  divided
1 (10-ounce) can Ro-Tel
  tomatoes and green chiles
Cheese strips for garnish

Cook rice and set aside. Cut peppers in half lengthwise and clean. Place in cold water and bring to a boil for 5 minutes; drain. Brown ground beef and onion; drain. Add salt and pepper to taste. Add cooked rice and 1 can tomato sauce; simmer for 5 minutes. Place peppers in Pyrex dish. Stuff peppers with meat mixture. Pour remaining can of tomato sauce and Ro-Tel tomatoes over and around peppers. Bake at 425º for 30–45 minutes. Place a strip of cheese on top of each pepper. Bake until cheese melts.

Ann McCoy (Book 3)

Mamie's Squash Pickles

12 squash, thinly sliced
2 bell peppers, chopped
2 onions, chopped
1 (3-ounce) jar pimentos, chopped
¼ cup salt

4 cups sugar
1 cup vinegar
1 teaspoon flour
2 teaspoons celery seed
1 teaspoon mustard seed

Combine squash, bell peppers, onions, and pimentos. Pour salt over squash medley; mix well and let set for 1 hour. Mix sugar, vinegar, flour, and spices; bring to a boil. Drain squash; add vinegar mixture and bring to a boil; cook for 20 minutes. Pour in jars and seal.

Gail Self, Greenwood Council (Book 1)

Sweet and Hot Garlic Pickles

This is delicious on peas and other vegetables or just eaten alone.

1 quart sliced dill pickles
1 clove garlic, chopped

2 cups sugar
⅓ (2-ounce) bottle Tabasco

Drain liquid from pickles. Add garlic, sugar, and Tabasco. Refrigerate. Pickles will be ready in 4 days. You will need to turn jar upside down each day as the sugar turns into liquid so the pickles will be well coated. If liquid doesn't cover all pickles, may need to add more sugar.

Faye Barlow, Jackson, MS (Book 4)

Oven Canned Tomatoes

Tomatoes (ripe)   Salt
Quart jars

Wash, peel, and core tomatoes. Pack in quart jars. (Do not add water.) Be sure juice covers the tomatoes. Add 1 teaspoon of salt to each jar (sprinkle salt on top of tomatoes). Seal jars; put in cold oven on bottom rack. Remove the top rack. Turn oven on to 200°. Cook 2 hours. (Do not open oven door during process.) After cooking for 2 hours, take out of oven and cover until jars cool, or turn off oven and leave jars in until cool.

Frances Barnes, Tupelo Life Member Club (Book 4)

Chow Chow

12 large onions   ½ cup salt
12 sweet green bell peppers   5 cups sugar
12 sweet red bell peppers   2 quarts vinegar
1 gallon chopped cabbage   6 tablespoons dry mustard
2 quarts chopped green   1 tablespoon turmeric
   tomatoes   1 tablespoon ginger
1 pint chopped celery   2 tablespoons pickling spices

Peel onions. Cut bell peppers and remove the seeds. Cut cabbage, tomatoes, and celery into pieces. Process through the medium knife of the food chopper; mix with salt and allow to stand in refrigerator overnight; drain.

Combine sugar, vinegar, mustard, turmeric, and ginger; add pickling spices in a spice bag. Bring mixture to a boil in a large stockpot and simmer gently for 5 minutes. Add vegetables and return to a boil; simmer for 5 minutes. Remove the spice bag and pack Chow Chow into hot sterilized jars. Seal at once.

Chris Reno, Jackson South Council (Book 2)

Pasta, Rice, Etc.

1930
Single Handset
Oval-Base

Although the single handset containing both the receiver and transmitter was developed for operators and repairmen by 1878, it wasn't until 1927 that the single handset telephone was introduced to the general public. The 1927 model had a round base. In 1930 it was redesigned with an elongated base made to compliment the long handset. The dial was also recessed into the front of the phone. Like the Candlestick, only the switchhook and switch were contained in the phone. The network and ringer were contained in a subset that was mounted on the wall. The subsets contained a new induction coil that would be used for nearly twenty years.

Cheesie Macaroni and Cheese

2 tablespoons oil
2 pounds elbow noodles or
  Barilla Cellentani pasta
1 pound medium Cheddar
  cheese
1 pound Monterey Jack cheese

1 (2-pound) block Velveeta
  cheese
2–2½ cups milk
4 eggs, beaten
Salt and pepper to taste
2 sticks butter

In a large stockpot with 2 tablespoons oil, boil noodles till al dente, approximately 12–14 minutes. Rinse and let drain well.

Shred Cheddar and Monterey Jack cheese and mix together. Slice Velveeta cheese into 2-inch cubes for easier melting, into a glass bowl. Add 2 cups milk. Heat slowly in the microwave, stirring frequently. Add more milk, if needed, to make a thin pancake batter consistency. After microwaving, fold in beaten eggs.

Spray large glass or metal deep-dish pan with nonstick spray. Layer bottom of pan with layer of noodles. Salt and pepper lightly. Slice 5–6 pieces of butter about ⅛ or ¼ inch thick and place across noodles. Layer on Cheddar and Monterey Jack cheese. Spoon on several ladle-size spoonfuls of Velveeta cheese sauce over this layer. Repeat the above until your pan is full, ending with Cheddar and Monterey Jack cheese. Try to leave about ¼ inch at the top of the pan. Bake in preheated 375° oven on top rack, uncovered, for 30–35 minutes or until brown.

OPTIONAL TOPPING:
8–10 slices white bread
2 sticks butter

1 bottle Hormel bacon bits

Toast well 8–10 slices white bread and crumble into bread crumbs. Melt 2 sticks butter. Mix bread crumbs and butter with 1 bottle Hormel bacon bits. Spread thin layer over the top of macaroni and cheese during the last 15–20 minutes of baking. Allow to brown. Let stand for a few minutes to thicken.

Betty Byrd, Jackson, MS (Book 4)

Macaroni Casserole

1 (8-ounce) package elbow
  macaroni, cooked in salt
  water and drained
¼ cup chopped bell pepper
¼ cup finely chopped pimentos
⅓ cup chopped onion
3 tablespoons margarine,
  melted
1 (10¾-ounce) can cream of
  mushroom soup
1 (4-ounce) can sliced
  mushrooms, drained
1 cup mayonnaise
¾ cup grated sharp Cheddar
  cheese
Bread crumbs with melted butter

Mix all ingredients together, except bread crumbs with butter, and put in buttered casserole dish. Top with bread crumbs. Bake for 20 minutes at 375º.

Jessie H. Rollins, Capitol Life Member Club (Book 1)

Chicken Tetrazzini

1 (6-ounce) package thin
  spaghetti
1 bunch green onions, chopped
  fine (use tops, too)
1 medium green bell pepper,
  chopped
Butter
2 cups cooked, boned chicken
1 (6-ounce) can sliced
  mushrooms
¼ cup chopped pimentos
½ teaspoon garlic powder
½ teaspoon salt
1 (10¾-ounce) can cream of
  mushroom soup
½ pint whipping cream
1 cup milk
1 cup grated sharp Cheddar
  cheese

While spaghetti cooks, brown onions and green bell pepper in butter. When onions are tender, add other ingredients, except spaghetti and cheese. Cook until well blended. Add spaghetti. Pour into greased casserole (or casseroles) and cook at 300º for 1 hour. Sprinkle cheese on top; turn off oven and let cheese melt. Yields 8–10 servings.

Polly Dickerson, Tupelo Council Life Member (Book 1)

Chicken Spaghetti

1 hen
2 (12-ounce) boxes spaghetti
5 medium onions, chopped
5 green peppers, chopped
1 (4-ounce) can sliced
   mushrooms, drained
5 tablespoons Wesson oil
1 (6-ounce) can tomato paste

2 (16-ounce) cans or 1 quart
   tomatoes
3 tablespoons sugar
1 (15-ounce) can English peas,
   drained
Salt and black pepper to taste
Red pepper to taste
1 pound Cheddar cheese, grated

You will need a large pot as this makes a large quantity. In salted water, boil hen until tender. Remove all bones and skin, and return chopped meat to broth. Cook spaghetti in salted water until tender. While spaghetti is cooking, brown onions, peppers, and mushrooms in oil. Add these with tomato paste, tomatoes, and sugar, to chicken and broth. Bring to a boil, then reduce heat and simmer. When spaghetti is tender, drain and add to chicken mixture. Stir in peas. Season to taste with salt, black pepper, and red pepper. About 30 minutes before serving, add cheese. Enjoy!

Variation: For a small family, fix the sauce with everything except the peas, spaghetti, and cheese. Divide into the quantity needed for your family, and freeze. When ready to serve, cook spaghetti, add thawed chicken mixture, 1 (8-ounce) can of peas, and 4 ounces grated cheese.

Fay Lambert, Greenwood Council (Book 1)

Spaghetti in One Pot

1 pound ground beef
1 medium onion, chopped
1 clove garlic, crushed
2 teaspoons salt
¼ teaspoon pepper
1 teaspoon oregano
1 teaspoon sweet basil
1 tablespoon prepared mustard
1 (8-ounce) package spaghetti,
  broken into fourths

3 cups tomato juice
1 (8-ounce) can tomato sauce
¼ cup brown sugar
1 (8-ounce) can sliced
  mushrooms, drained (optional)
1 cup (4 ounces) cubed Cheddar
  cheese
Grated Parmesan cheese
  (optional)

Combine ground beef, onion, and garlic in a 2-quart saucepan; cook until meat is browned and onion is tender; drain. Add salt, pepper, oregano, basil, and mustard; stir. Add spaghetti, tomato juice, tomato sauce, and sugar. Cook 15 minutes or until spaghetti is tender, stirring occasionally. Add mushrooms, if desired, and Cheddar cheese; stir. Serve topped with Parmesan cheese, if desired. Yields 5–6 servings.

Dot Trinkner, Jackson North Council (Book 1)

Lasagna

1 package lasagna noodles
1 pound ground beef or chuck
1 tablespoon salad oil
1 garlic clove, minced
1 tablespoon plus 2 teaspoons
  parsley flakes, divided
4 teaspoons salt, divided
1 (14-ounce) can tomatoes
1 (6-ounce) can tomato paste
2 eggs, beaten
2 (12-ounce) cartons cottage
  cheese
½ teaspoon pepper
½ cup grated Parmesan cheese
1 pound mozzarella cheese,
  sliced or grated

Cook lasagna noodles in boiling salted water; drain and rinse. Brown meat in oil; add garlic, 1 tablespoon parsley flakes, 2 teaspoons salt, tomatoes, and tomato paste. Simmer 30 minutes to 1 hour. Mix eggs, remaining 2 teaspoons parsley flakes, remaining 2 teaspoons salt, cottage cheese, pepper, and Parmesan cheese in bowl and set aside. Place a layer of noodles in greased 9x13x2-inch pan or dish. Cover with half cottage cheese-Parmesan mixture; add half mozzarella cheese, then half of meat mixture. Repeat for second layer. Bake at 375º for 30 minutes.

Leo and Margie Pullen, Gulf Coast Council (Book 2)

Inside Out Ravioli

1 (6-ounce) package wide egg
  noodles
2 packages frozen chopped
  spinach
2 eggs, well beaten
1 pound sharp Cheddar cheese,
  grated

1½ pounds ground round
1 large onion, chopped
Salt and pepper to taste
1 (1-pound) jar Ragu spaghetti
  sauce
1 (8-ounce) can tomato paste

Cook the noodles and spinach (separately) according to package directions. Drain the noodles and place in a large bowl. Drain the spinach, reserving liquid. Add the spinach to the noodles along with eggs and grated cheese. Place in a greased 9x13-inch casserole dish. Brown meat and onion; drain if necessary. Add salt and pepper to taste. Add the spaghetti sauce and tomato paste along with reserved spinach liquid and simmer 20 minutes. Pour sauce over noodle mixture and bake at 350º for 30 minutes. Let it sit about 5 minutes before serving. Yields 8–10 servings.

Carolyn Little, Greenwood Council (Book 1)

The first telephone exchange in Mississippi was opened in Vicksburg on January 10, 1881, and was one of the first in the South. This was eight months prior to Atlanta, the present headquarters of BellSouth, receiving a telephone exchange.

Beef Stuffed Manicotti

4 manicotti shells, cooked in
  salted water for 10 minutes
½ pound ground chuck
1 small onion, finely chopped
½ bell pepper, finely chopped
1 (15-ounce) can tomato sauce

1–1½ teaspoons dried oregano
1 teaspoon thyme
1 bay leaf
1 cup shredded mozzarella
  cheese, divided

Set aside cooked manicotti shells. Sauté ground chuck, onion, and bell pepper until brown; drain if necessary. Add tomato sauce, oregano, thyme, and bay leaf; simmer on low heat for about 10 minutes. Remove bay leaf. Add ½ cup cheese and stir until it is melted. Arrange shells in a casserole dish and stuff with half of meat mixture. Pour remaining meat mixture over shells; sprinkle with remaining ½ cup cheese. Bake at 300º for 30 minutes. Double if you are serving more than 2 people.

J. K. Culipher, Jackson South Council (Book 2)

Rice Casserole

1 cup rice, uncooked
½ cup vegetable oil
1 cup diced sharp Cheddar
  cheese
1 (½-ounce) jar stuffed olives,
  chopped

1 (10-ounce) can Ro-Tel
  tomatoes
½ cup chopped onion
1 cup water
Salt and pepper to taste

Mix all ingredients and place in lightly greased casserole dish. Cover and cook at 350° for 1 hour.

Jaunita R. Verucchi, Jackson North Council (Book 2)

Garden Rice

1 bunch green onions, chopped
1 bell pepper, chopped
1½ pounds fresh squash, sliced
4 tablespoons butter
1 (12-ounce) can Mexicorn, drained
½ teaspoon coriander
1 teaspoon salt
1 teaspoon lemon pepper
¾ teaspoon oregano
1 teaspoon parsley flakes
1½ cup rice, cooked
½ cup butter, melted

Sauté onions, bell pepper, and squash in butter until tender. Add corn, coriander, salt, lemon pepper, oregano, and parsley. Place drained rice in large bowl; pour melted butter over and toss lightly. Combine vegetables with rice; toss. Place in buttered casserole dish and cover. Heat in 350º oven for 15 minutes. Serves 10–12.

Willie Allen Williams, Clarksdale Club (Book 1)

Green Rice Casserole

2 (10-ounce) packages frozen chopped broccoli
1 onion, chopped
1 cup chopped celery
1 stick margarine
2 cups cooked rice
2 (10¾-ounce) cans cream of mushroom soup
1 (8-ounce) jar Cheez Whiz (can use jalapeño flavor)

Cook broccoli according to package directions; drain and set aside. Sauté onion and celery in margarine. Combine all ingredients. Mix well and pour into buttered casserole. Bake 45 minutes at 325º. This may be frozen.

Billie Sue Rouse, Jackson North Council (Book 1)

Spanish Tomato Rice

8 slices bacon
1 cup finely chopped onions
¼ cup chopped bell pepper
1 (16-ounce) can diced tomatoes
1½ cups water
¾ cup uncooked long-grain
  rice

½ cup chili sauce
1 teaspoon salt
1 teaspoon brown sugar
½ teaspoon Worcestershire
Dash of black pepper

In a 10-inch skillet, cook bacon until crisp; set aside and reserve half the grease. In the remaining grease, sauté onions and bell pepper until tender, but not brown. Add tomatoes, water, rice, chili sauce, salt, brown sugar, Worcestershire, and pepper. Cover and simmer 35–40 minutes. Crumble bacon on top. Serves 6.

Bubbles Talbot, Gulf Coast Council (Book 2)

Sausage Rice Casserole

Good also for stuffing peppers.

2 (16-ounce) rolls sausage,
  hot or mild, chopped
2 cups water
1 (1-ounce) package dry Lipton
  chicken-rice soup mix

¾ cup finely chopped celery
¾ cup finely chopped onion
¾ cup finely chopped green
  bell pepper
3 cups cooked rice

Brown sausage in skillet; drain. Boil water; add soup mix and simmer about 5 minutes. Add celery, onion, and bell pepper; simmer about 5 minutes more or until tender. Combine both mixtures together with rice. Bake at 400º for 15–20 minutes.

Gail Rushing, Natchez Council (Book 2)

Cajun Red Beans and Rice

1 pound dried red beans
1 meaty ham bone
3 green onions, sliced
1 large onion, chopped
1 large clove garlic, minced
1 stalk celery, chopped

1 bay leaf
1 tablespoon chopped parsley
Salt and pepper to taste
1 pound Creole or Polish
   sausage, cut into small pieces
Cooked rice

Wash and sort beans; put in large pot and cover with water. Bring to a boil and boil rapidly for 2 minutes. Turn off fire and let beans sit covered for 1 hour. Bring beans to a boil again, then lower heat. Add ham bone, green onions, chopped onion, garlic, celery, bay leaf, parsley, salt and pepper. Cook slowly for 2–3 hours. Add the sausage the last hour. Add about a cup of water toward the end of cooking if the mixture gets too dry. Stir frequently and scrape down the sides and across the bottom of pot with wooden spoon to prevent scorching. Stir the entire mixture about every 30 minutes. Serve over cooked rice.

Bertha P. Smith, Jackson North Council (Book 2)

Red Beans and Rice

1 pound dried red beans
¼ pound salt pork
1 smoked ham hock
2 quarts water
3 yellow onions, chopped
1 bunch green onions, chopped
1 green bell pepper, chopped
2 large garlic cloves, minced
2 cups chopped fresh parsley
½ teaspoon cayenne pepper
½ teaspoon black pepper
2 bay leaves
¼ teaspoon oregano
¼ teaspoon thyme
1 tablespoon Worcestershire
½ teaspoon hot pepper sauce
2 pounds smoked sausage
1 (8-ounce) can tomato sauce
4 cups cooked long-grain rice

Rinse and sort beans. Soak overnight. Cook beans, salt pork, and ham hock in 2 quarts water for 1½ hours in a very large pot.

In skillet, sauté yellow onions, green onions, bell pepper, and garlic until tender. Add this to the beans, along with parsley, spices, Worcestershire, and hot sauce.

Brown sliced sausage. Drain; add to the beans. Add tomato sauce. Cook 2–3 hours more, stirring often, adding water as needed. Serve over cooked rice.

Kathy Wilder, Jackson, MS (Book 4)

Meats

1937
"300" Series

An innovation in telephone design was the placing of the bell in the base of the "300" Series desk set. The "300" Series was the first model that included the ringer, coil, and capacitor in the base, forming a complete phone in one package. Previous models required an external subset that contained these components. The "300" Series was made from 1936 until 1954. Earlier versions had housings made of die-cast metal but thermo-plastic was substituted in the early 1940s due to the onset of World War II.

Soon crossbar switching was introduced, and automation came to long-distance switching. Dialed routing codes soon gave way to the familiar area codes, which the switch itself could translate into the needed routing information. Call completion time dropped to 10–20 seconds.

Salisbury Steak

HORSERADISH SAUCE:

1½ tablespoons bread crumbs
3 tablespoons whipping cream
1½ tablespoons grated fresh
  horseradish

Salt and pepper to taste
Dash of dry mustard
1½ teaspoons vinegar

Combine all ingredients; cook over low heat until sauce is thoroughly heated. Keep warm until ready to serve.

½ pound lean ground beef
1 tablespoon onion juice

½ teaspoon salt
Dash of black pepper

Combine ground beef, onion juice, salt and pepper; mix thoroughly. Shape into patties. Broil patties 3–6 minutes on each side or to desired doneness. Serve immediately with Horseradish Sauce.

Eurcle Culipher, Jackson North Council (Book 2)

Spaghetti Meat Sauce

1½ pounds ground beef
½ cup chopped celery
½ cup chopped green bell
  pepper
¾ cup chopped onion
1½ teaspoons chili powder

1 teaspoon curry powder
1 tablespoon garlic salt
1 teaspoon black pepper
½ teaspoon red pepper
1 (12-ounce) can tomato juice
2 (6-ounce) cans tomato paste

Brown ground beef in a little hot fat until browned; drain. Add celery, bell pepper, onion, and spices. Cook for about 10 minutes. Add tomato juice (if you like it "soupier," add more juice) and tomato paste; cook until very thick. Takes about 1 hour or more. Serve with hot pasta of your choice. Sprinkle heavily with grated cheese just before serving.

Frances Barnes, Tupelo Life Member Club (Book 3)

Spiced Meatballs

1 pound ground beef	¾ cup seasoned bread crumbs
½ teaspoon Ac'cent	1 tablespoon ketchup
¼ teaspoon pepper	4 drops hot sauce
½ teaspoon salt	1 tablespoon grated Parmesan
2 eggs, well beaten	cheese
2 tablespoons finely chopped	2–3 tablespoons butter
onion	

Mix well all ingredients except butter, and shape into 1-inch balls. Sauté meatballs in butter until brown. Drain well and set aside.

SAUCE:

3 tablespoons butter or	2 tablespoons finely chopped
margarine	onion
½ cup ketchup	2 tablespoons Worcestershire
½ cup chili sauce	1 teaspoon Ac'cent
¼ cup cider vinegar	4 drops hot sauce
½ cup brown sugar	¼ teaspoon pepper

Combine ingredients in large saucepan and bring to a boil. Reduce heat and simmer 5 minutes. Add meatballs and simmer 10 minutes more.

Joyce Moore, Jackson South Council (Book 1)

Sicilian Meat Roll

2 eggs, beaten
¾ cup soft bread crumbs
½ cup tomato juice
2 tablespoons snipped parsley
½ teaspoon crushed oregano
¼ teaspoon salt
¼ teaspoon pepper

1 clove garlic, minced
2 pounds lean ground beef
8 thin slices boiled ham
1½ cups shredded mozzarella
   cheese
3 slices mozzarella cheese, cut
   in halves on diagonal

Combine eggs, bread crumbs, tomato juice, parsley, oregano, salt, pepper, and garlic. Stir in ground beef, mixing well. On foil or wax paper, pat meat into a 12x10-inch rectangle. Arrange ham slices atop meat, leaving a small margin around edges. Sprinkle shredded cheese over ham. Starting from the short end, carefully roll up meat, using foil to lift; seal edges and ends. Place roll seam side down in baking dish and bake in 350º oven for 1 hour and 15 minutes or until done. Place cheese wedges over the top of the roll and return to oven for 5 minutes or until cheese melts.

Lynda Smith, Gulf Coast Council (Book 2)

The first long-distance line in Mississippi was between Vicksburg and Jackson, and was built in 1883.

Meatloaf with Pecan Stuffing

PECAN STUFFING:

1 egg, slightly beaten
¼ cup oil
2 cups whole-wheat bread
  crumbs

½ cup chopped celery
¼ teaspoon black pepper
½ cup meat stock or water
½ cup chopped pecans

Combine egg, oil, whole-wheat crumbs, celery, black pepper, meat stock, and chopped pecans. Set aside.

MEATLOAF:

1½ pounds lean ground beef
½ cup chopped bell pepper
⅓ cup chopped onion
1 tablespoon Worcestershire

Salt to taste
1 cup white bread crumbs
½ cup milk
1 egg, slightly beaten

Combine beef with bell pepper, onion, Worcestershire, salt, white bread crumbs, milk, and egg. Mix thoroughly. Place ½ of mixture in bottom of greased loaf pan.

Spread Pecan Stuffing on top of the meat mixture. Arrange the second half of the meat mixture on top of stuffing. Bake at 350º for 1½ hours and cool slightly before removing from pan.

Dora T. Tidwell, Tupelo Council (Book 2)

Savory Frosted Meatloaf

2 pounds ground beef
½ cup Kraft French dressing
1 teaspoon salt
¼ teaspoon pepper
½ cup dry bread crumbs
½ cup chopped onion
3 eggs, divided

2 cups hot mashed potatoes
½ cup Miracle Whip salad
  dressing
Broiled mushrooms
Pimento strips
Parsley

Combine meat, French dressing, salt, pepper, bread crumbs, onion, and 2 beaten eggs. Shape into oval loaf. Place in shallow baking dish; bake at 350º for 1 hour. Place on baking sheet or heat-proof platter. Combine potatoes, remaining beaten egg, and Miracle Whip; frost loaf. Broil until lightly browned. Garnish with mushrooms, pimento, and parsley. Makes 6–8 servings.

Frances W. Caffey (Book 3)

Ground Beef Casserole

2 pounds ground beef
1 onion, chopped
Salt and pepper to taste
1 (11-ounce) can shoe peg corn,
  drained
½ cup chopped pimentos
1 (10¾-ounce) can cream of
  chicken soup

1 (10¾-ounce) can cream of
  mushroom soup
1 (8-ounce) carton sour cream
1 (5½-ounce) package noodles,
  cooked and drained
Cracker crumbs and butter
  for topping

Brown meat and onion together in a skillet; drain; salt and pepper to taste. Mix with corn, pimentos, soups, and sour cream. Rinse the soup can with a small amount of water and add to the mixture. Add noodles. Pour into a greased casserole dish. Top with cracker crumbs and dot with butter. Bake at 350º for 30 minutes. Serves 12.

Carolyn Little, Greenwood Council (Book 2)

Mashed Potato Beef Casserole

2 strips bacon, diced
1 pound ground beef
1 large onion, finely chopped
¼ pound fresh mushrooms,
   sliced
1 large carrot, finely chopped
1 celery stalk, finely chopped
3 tablespoons flour

1 cup beef broth
1 tablespoon Worcestershire
1 teaspoon dried tarragon
¼ teaspoon pepper
3 cups hot mashed potatoes
¾ cup shredded Cheddar
   cheese, divided
Paprika

Cook bacon until crisp; drain, and set aside; reserve 1 teaspoon drippings. Cook beef in drippings over medium heat until no longer pink; drain. Toss onion, mushrooms, carrot, and celery in flour; add to meat in skillet along with broth, Worcestershire, tarragon, and pepper. Bring to a boil; reduce heat. Simmer, uncovered, 15–20 minutes or until vegetables are tender. Add bacon; transfer to a greased 2-quart baking dish.

Combine potatoes and ½ cup cheese; spread over the beef mixture. Sprinkle with paprika and remaining ¼ cup cheese. Bake, uncovered, at 350º for 20–25 minutes or until heated through. Broil 4 inches from heat 5 minutes or until bubbly. Yields 4–6 servings.

Bess Lancaster, Grenada, MS (Book 4)

Hamburger Pie

1 medium onion, chopped	1 tablespoon Worcestershire
1 pound ground beef	1 (15-ounce) can Veg-All
1 tablespoon salt	1 (15-ounce) can tomato sauce
¼ teaspoon pepper	¼ cup grated sharp Cheddar
¼ teaspoon chili powder	cheese

Brown onion and beef; drain. In a greased casserole dish, combine beef mixture, seasonings, Veg-All, and tomato sauce. Top with cheese. Bake at 350º for 30 minutes, or until heated thoroughly.

Sweet Pea Dees, Jackson South Council (Book 2)

Cheeseburger Casserole

1 pound ground beef	1 (8-ounce) can tomato sauce
¼ cup chopped onion	8 ounces American cheese,
¾ teaspoon salt	sliced and cut in thin strips
⅛ teaspoon pepper	1 (10-ounce) can refrigerator
¼ cup ketchup	biscuits

Combine beef and onion in skillet. Cook until beef is lightly brown; drain. Add salt and pepper. Stir in ketchup and tomato sauce. Heat thoroughly. Turn into 1½-quart casserole dish. Sprinkle cheese over beef mixture. Top with biscuits. Bake at 425º for 10–15 minutes or until golden brown. Serves 4–6.

Ethel H. Barlow, Jackson South Council (Book 1)

Blue Cheese Burgers

2 pounds lean ground beef
⅓ cup chopped onion
⅓ cup crumbled blue cheese
1 tablespoon Worcestershire

2 teaspoons salt
1 loaf French bread
½ cup butter, softened
¼ cup prepared mustard

Combine ground beef, onion, blue cheese, Worcestershire, and salt. Shape into 10 oval patties, slightly larger than diameter of the French bread. Cut French loaf in 20 half-inch slices. Blend butter and mustard; spread generously on one side of each slice. Reassemble loaf, buttered sides together. Wrap in heavy foil; place on grill over medium coals (about 15 minutes). Broil burgers 5–6 minutes; turn and broil other side about 5 minutes. Serve on hot French loaf. So good!

Bubbles Talbot, Gulf Coast Council (Book 2)

Sloppy Joe Burgers

1½ pounds ground beef
1 large onion, chopped
1 bell pepper, chopped
1 teaspoon vegetable or
    olive oil

¾ cup ketchup
1 tablespoon sugar
1 tablespoon prepared mustard
1 tablespoon vinegar
1 teaspoon salt

Brown beef, onion, and bell pepper in hot oil. Drain. Add remaining ingredients and simmer for 30 minutes. Serve over warm buns.

Billie Buford, Oakland, MS (Book 4)

Greco

1 pound ground beef	2 cups cooked macaroni shells
1 small onion, chopped	2 (15-ounce) cans tomato sauce
1 small green bell pepper,	1 (10-ounce) can cream corn
chopped	Salt to taste
Mushrooms (optional)	Grated sharp Cheddar cheese

Brown ground beef, onion, and pepper; drain. Add mushrooms, if desired, macaroni, tomato sauce, and corn. Season to taste. Mix well and place in casserole dish. Cover with cheese and bake for 1 hour at 300º.

Dianne Fagan Rainey, Hattiesburg RSSC (Book 3)

Hasty Tamale Casserole

2 (15-ounce) cans tamales	1 (15-ounce) can chili without
1 pound ground chuck	beans
Salt and pepper to taste	1 cup grated sharp Cheddar
1 medium onion, chopped	cheese
1 large jalapeño pepper, seeded	1 (8-ounce) package corn chips,
and chopped	crushed

Line the bottom of an oiled, 1-quart loaf pan with tamales, side by side. In a skillet, brown ground beef, separating with a fork while browning; drain fat. Add salt and pepper. Over tamales, layer meat, onion, jalapeño, and chili. Sprinkle top with cheese and corn chips. Bake at 350º for 30–40 minutes or until bubbly. Serves 4.

Ann McCoy (Book 3)

Enchilada Casserole

12 corn tortillas, divided
1 pound ground beef,
  browned and drained
1 teaspoon salt
2 tablespoons chili powder
1 medium onion, chopped
1 (15-ounce) can Ranch Style
  beans

½ pound Velveeta cheese,
  sliced
1 (10¾-ounce) can cream of
  chicken soup
1 (10-ounce) can Ro-Tel
  tomatoes, drained

Place 6 tortillas on bottom of 9x13-inch pan. Layer in order on tortillas: beef seasoned with salt, chili powder, onion, beans, and cheese. Top with remaining tortillas, soup, and tomatoes. Bake 1 hour in 380º oven.

Theresa Buchanan (Book 3)

Grilled Fajitas

2 pounds steak
1½ cups red wine vinegar
1 cup water
2 teaspoons salt
½ teaspoon pepper
2 cloves garlic, chopped

4 green chiles, chopped
½ cup red wine
1 teaspoon oregano
1 teaspoon cumin
1 teaspoon paprika

Place steaks in glass container; combine all other ingredients and pour over steaks. Marinate overnight. Wrap in foil. Cook on grill about 20 minutes. Remove from foil and brown on each side. Cut in strips against the grain. Serve with flour tortillas and guacamole or vegetables of your choice.

Kyla Moore, Meridian, MS (Book 4)

London Broil

¼ cup ketchup	1 teaspoon dry mustard
⅓ cup red wine vinegar	1 tablespoon Worcestershire
¼ cup brown sugar	1 teaspoon garlic powder
¼ cup white wine	1 stick butter
2 tablespoons soy sauce	1 flank steak

Blend ingredients to make marinade and pour ¾ of marinade over steak. Marinate in refrigerator for a minimum of 3 hours. Grill steak 5–10 minutes on each side, according to your taste. Baste with the remaining ¼ of marinade during grilling. Serve sliced in thin pieces, cutting on the diagonal.

Krisha Wren, Ponotoc, MS (Book 4)

Beef Stroganoff

1½ pounds round steak or stew meat	½ cup chopped onion
¼ cup flour	1 small clove garlic, minced
Dash of pepper	1 (10-ounce) can beef broth,
¼ cup butter	or 3 bouillon cubes in 3 cups water
1 (4-ounce) can sliced mushrooms, drained	1 cup sour cream
	Cooked noodles or rice

Cut meat into thin strips; dust with flour and pepper. In large skillet, brown meat in butter. Add mushrooms, onion, and garlic; brown lightly. Stir in beef broth. Cover and cook 1 hour, stirring now and then. Gradually stir in sour cream. Cook over low heat 5 minutes. Serve over noodles or rice.

Willie Allen Williams, Clarksdale Club (Book 1)

French Quarter Steak

1 pound boneless round steak
¼ cup all-purpose flour
1 teaspoon salt
2 teaspoons paprika
½ teaspoon pepper
¾ cup chopped onion

⅓ cup chopped bell pepper
2 tablespoons vegetable oil
½ cup uncooked rice
1 (28-ounce) can tomatoes,
    undrained
1 cup water

Trim excess fat from steak; cut steak into serving pieces. Combine flour, salt, paprika, and pepper. Coat steak in flour mixture; reserve excess mixture. Sauté onion and bell pepper in hot oil in large skillet; remove vegetables; set aside. Brown steak on both sides in remaining oil in skillet; add sautéed vegetables, rice, tomatoes, and water. Sprinkle with reserved flour mixture; cover and simmer 1 hour, stirring occasionally.

Mary "Charlie" Roach, Jackson South Council (Book 2)

Roast

1 (4- to 5-pound) rump roast,
    sirloin tip roast, or any cut
    you prefer

Garlic powder to taste
Black pepper to taste

Rub roast with garlic powder and black pepper.

MARINADE:

¼ cup soy sauce
¼ cup Worcestershire
½ teaspoon sugar

1 teaspoon liquid smoke
1 teaspoon Louisiana hot sauce
1 tablespoon onion powder

Mix Marinade ingredients and pour over roast. Marinate overnight and put in crockpot on LOW to cook all day.

Sheila Moore, Jackson Council (Book 3)

Roast Beef with Horseradish Sauce

1 (3½-pound) eye of round roast	2 teaspoons seasoned pepper
2 tablespoons prepared mustard	2 cloves garlic, crushed
	2 teaspoons dried thyme leaves

Place roast, fat side down, in microwave-safe baking pan with roasting rack. Brush mustard on meat surface. In small bowl, combine seasonings and pat evenly on roast.

Cover the ends of the roast, leaving center uncovered and cook on HIGH for 5 minutes, then rotate dish and remove covering. For medium-rare roast, cook another 20 minutes on MEDIUM. Let stand for 5 minutes.

HORSERADISH CREAM SAUCE:

½ cup heavy cream	2 tablespoons prepared horseradish
¼ cup sour cream	⅛ teaspoon salt
1 teaspoon prepared mustard	

In a small bowl, beat heavy cream until stiff peaks form. In another bowl, combine sour cream, mustard, horseradish, and salt; mix well. Fold in whipped cream. Slice roast and serve with Horseradish Cream Sauce.

Debby Ivy (Book 3)

Working Person's Roast

1 roast (beef or pork, any size)
3 cloves garlic, slivered
1 (10¾-ounce) can cream of
  mushroom soup

2 tablespoons Worcestershire
Salt and pepper to taste
1 package Lipton Onion Soup
  mix

Place roast in center of large sheet of aluminum foil. Cut slits in roast and push in garlic. Pour mushroom soup over roast, then Worcestershire. Sprinkle dry soup mix over roast. Add salt and pepper to taste. Pull foil up around roast, sealing tightly, leaving a little room around the meat. Cook in 250° oven all day from 7 a.m. to 5 p.m.

Fran Douglas, Jackson, MS (Book 4)

Shredded Beef

1 (6- to 7-pound) boneless,
  well trimmed beef roast
1 bay leaf
1 tablespoon oregano

1 tablespoon summer savory
1 tablespoon peppercorns
1 tablespoon rosemary
1 tablespoon garlic salt

Place roast in Dutch oven or crockpot with tight fitting lid. Half cover with water. Add spices and cook (Dutch oven 250° or crock-pot on HIGH) all day or until meat shreds. Remove from pot; shred with 2 forks. Serve open-faced on pumpernickel or rye bread with Sauce on the side. Serves 12.

SAUCE:
1 (2-ounce) can dry mustard
1 cup vinegar

2 eggs
1 cup sugar

Combine dry mustard and vinegar; let stand overnight. Beat eggs and place in double boiler; add sugar and mustard mixture. Cook over hot water, stirring until it thickens like gravy.

Mrs. Clyde Manning, Greenwood Council (Book 2)

Fall-Apart Tender Slow Roast Pork

Turnip greens are the perfect side-dish for pork butt roast.

1 (4-pound) pork butt roast
¼–⅓ cup Worcestershire
¾ cup light brown sugar

1 cup pasteurized apple juice
½ teaspoon salt

With a shelf arranged slightly below the center, preheat oven to 400°. Place pork in a casserole dish just large enough to hold it, and one that has an oven-proof lid. Sprinkle pork on all sides with Worcestershire, then press sugar coating on all sides of pork. Pour apple juice in the bottom of the casserole dish. Do not pour over the meat. Cover tightly.

Place pork in oven and turn oven down to 200°; roast, without opening the oven for about 5 hours, until meat is so tender that it literally falls apart. If meat does not fall apart easily, cover and return to oven and roast 30 minutes more. Sprinkle with salt. Do not omit this salt, it is vital for the taste of the dish. Serve hot or at room temperature.

Note: This can easily be done in the crockpot. Set on HIGH for 30 minutes, then turn down to LOW for the night or day.

Anna C. Nail, Grenada, MS (Book 4)

Heart Healthy Beef or Pork Stir-Fry

1 pound lean boneless beef top
  round or boneless pork loin,
  sliced in ¼-inch-thick strips
1 tablespoon vegetable oil
½ pound carrots, cut in ⅛-inch
  diagonal slices

½ pound fresh broccoli,
  flowerets separated and
  stems chopped
1 small onion, sliced
1 tablespoon soy sauce
1 clove garlic, minced (optional)

Trim excess fat from cuts. Quickly brown lean beef or pork strips in hot oil in large skillet, stirring constantly. Add carrots, broccoli stems, and onion. Cook until vegetables are hot, but crisp, stirring constantly. Add broccoli flowerets and soy sauce; stir 1 minute. Makes 4 servings.

Dot Trinkner (Book 3)

Spareribs

5 pounds lean spareribs or
  pork chops
Salt and pepper to taste
½ cup finely diced onion
¼ cup diced green bell pepper
1 tablespoon Worcestershire

2 (8-ounce) cans tomato sauce
⅓ cup cider or wine vinegar
1 (20-ounce) can pineapple
  tidbits with syrup
½ cup brown sugar
½ teaspoon dry mustard

Cut after every third rib about halfway down through the strip of spareribs. Sprinkle with salt and pepper. Place in shallow roasting pan. Bake in 350º oven for 1 hour and 25 minutes. Carefully drain off fat. While ribs are roasting, mix remaining ingredients and let stand to blend flavor. Pour over ribs or pork chops. Bake for 45–50 more minutes, basting frequently to coat ribs or pork chops with flavored sauce.

Annie L. Jones, Grenada Council (Book 3)

Pork Chops and Fried Rice Casserole

1¾ cups water
1½ cups Minute Rice
2 slices bacon
2 eggs, beaten
2 tablespoons water

¼ cup sliced green onions
 with tops
4 tablespoons soy sauce, divided
4 pork rib chops

In saucepan, bring 1¾ cups water to a boil. Remove from heat; stir in rice. Cover; set aside. In skillet, cook bacon until crisp. Remove bacon and crumble, reserving 2 tablespoons drippings. Set aside.

In bowl, combine eggs and 2 tablespoons water. In skillet, cook eggs in 1 tablespoon reserved drippings until set, stirring occasionally. Cut eggs in narrow strips. Add cooked rice, bacon, onions, and 3 tablespoons soy sauce to eggs; mix well. Turn into a greased 1½-quart casserole. In skillet, brown chops on both sides in remaining 1 tablespoon drippings. Arrange chops on top of rice mixture; brush with remaining 1 tablespoon soy sauce. Bake, covered, at 350° until chops are tender, about 40 minutes.

Melodye Wiggins, Gulf Coast Council (Book 1)

Pork Chop Casserole

6–8 center-cut pork chops,
  seasoned

6–8 medium potatoes, peeled
  and thinly sliced

1 (15-ounce) can English peas,
  drained

1 (15-ounce) can carrots, drained

Salt and pepper to taste

1 (10¾-ounce) can cream of
  onion soup

1 (10¾-ounce) can cream of
  celery soup

Place pork chops in bottom of 9x13-inch pan. Layer potatoes, peas, and carrots alternately until all are used. Add salt and pepper to taste. Pour both cans of soup over mixture. Cover with foil and bake in preheated 350º oven for 1 hour. Remove foil and bake another 10 minutes.

Gail Garner, Natchez Council and Mrs. W. G. Morgan (Buddy),
Greenwood Council (Book 2)

Skillet Pork Chops

4 thin-cut pork chops

1 tablespoon oil

2 medium onions, sliced
  lengthwise

1 clove garlic

½ cup beef broth

1 tablespoon soy sauce

1 teaspoon grated ginger

1 teaspoon brown sugar

In a large skillet, brown chops in oil; remove and set aside. In same skillet, sauté onions and garlic until lightly browned. Return chops to skillet. Add mixture of broth, soy sauce, ginger, and brown sugar; cover and cook over low heat 15–20 minutes or until chops are tender.

Frances D. Munn, Laurel Council (Book 1)

Ham Rice Skillet

2 cups cooked chopped ham
½ cup chopped onion
2 tablespoons butter or
  margarine
1 (8-ounce) can pineapple
  chunks

1 cup rice
½ cup brown sugar
2 tablespoons vinegar
1½ teaspoons salt

Cook ham and onion in butter in 10-inch skillet until onion is tender. Drain pineapple and reserve juice; add water to juice to make a total of 2½ cups liquid. Add liquid, pineapple, rice, brown sugar, vinegar, and salt to ham. Stir; bring to a boil. Reduce heat; cover and cook about 25 minutes or until liquid is absorbed. Makes 6 servings.

Mary R. Roach, Jackson South Council (Book 1)

Ham-Vegetable Pie

2 tablespoons margarine
3 cups cubed, cooked ham
1 medium onion, sliced
2 (10¾-ounce) cans cream of
  chicken soup

1 cup milk
1 (15-ounce) can Veg-All
1 (10-count) can biscuits

Heat oven to 425°. Melt margarine in large skillet. Cook ham and onions in margarine until onions are tender. Stir in soup and milk until smooth. Add Veg-All and heat just to boiling; stir frequently. Pour into ungreased 8x8x2-inch baking dish. Cut biscuits into quarters and place on top of mixture. Place in oven and bake, uncovered, for 10–15 minutes, or until biscuits are done. Makes 9–12 servings.

Gloria Brown, Paris, MS (Book 4)

Bryan's "Easy as Pie" Sausage Pie

¾ cup Bryan pork sausage,
  cooked and crumbled
1 cup shredded Swiss cheese
  or Cheddar cheese
⅓ cup chopped green onions
2 tablespoons chopped fresh
  parsley
2 ounces diced pimientos,
  well drained
4 eggs, beaten
2 cups milk
1 cup Bisquick baking mix
Salt and black or red pepper
  to taste

Cook sausage; crumble and drain well. Sprinkle sausage in bottom of quiche pan, 10½-inch pie plate or 9x13-inch baking dish that has been sprayed with cooking spray. Top with shredded cheese, onions, parsley, and pimiento. Mix eggs, milk, baking mix, salt, and pepper for 1 minute or until well blended and smooth. Pour into pie plate. Bake 35–40 minutes at 400° or until knife inserted in center comes out clean. Cool 5 minutes.

Barbara Staples, Laurel, MS (Book 4)

Venison Tenderloins

2 eggs
¼ cup milk
1 pound venison tenderloins,
  cut in serving-size pieces
1 cup cornflake crumbs
Salt and pepper to taste

Whip eggs and milk together. Dip tenderloins in mixture and coat with cornflake crumbs. Season with salt and pepper. Put in greased shallow pan and cook in 350° oven for 1 hour, turning once, when top sides are nicely browned. Serves 4.

Mildred Lauderdale, Greenwood Council (Book 1)

Veal Parmigiana

⅓ cup butter or margarine,
  melted
¾ teaspoon salt
⅛ teaspoon black pepper
1 cup bread crumbs
2 teaspoons oregano
½ cup grated Parmesan cheese
1 cup finely crushed cornflakes

1 (2 pound) veal cutlet, cut into
  6 pieces (can substitute steak)
2 eggs, slightly beaten
2 (8-ounce) cans tomato sauce
¼ teaspoon onion salt
½ cup sugar
6–8 slices mozzarella cheese

Pour melted butter in 9x13-inch pan. Blend salt, pepper, bread crumbs, oregano, Parmesan cheese, and cornflakes in a separate dish. Dip meat in eggs and then in crumb mixture, then in corn flakes. Place meat in buttered pan. Cook 20 minutes in 400º oven; turn and bake 20 minute on the other side. Mix tomato sauce, onion salt, and sugar and heat. Pour sauce around meat; top each piece with cheese. Return to oven to melt cheese slightly.

Karyl Duett, Meridian Council (Book 1)

Poultry

1954
"500" Series

With the invention of the transistor in 1947, the vacuum tube transmitter was soon replaced. Equipment size was reduced and reliability increased, making telephone service more affordable. The telephone started to become a decorative household item in the early 1950s. Although some colored telephones were available much earlier, they did not gain widespread popularity until the advent of the "500" color series. Besides black, the five basic colors available were white, beige, green, pink, and blue. Standard with all the sets was an adjustable volume control for the bell. An improved, more flexible neoprene jacketed telephone cord replaced the cotton covered cords used since telephony began. As many households began using more than one phone, the telephone returned to the wall in a companion piece to the "500" desk set. The wall set was most often used in the kitchen where counter and table space was at a premium.

Buttermilk Fried Chicken

½ cup all-purpose flour
¾ teaspoon salt
¼ teaspoon paprika
¼ teaspoon ground thyme
¼ teaspoon ground marjoram

Pinch of pepper
2 whole chicken breasts, split
½ cup buttermilk
Vegetable oil for frying

Combine first 6 ingredients; stir well. Dip each piece of chicken in buttermilk; dredge in flour mixture, coating well. Heat 1 inch of oil in a skillet; add chicken and cook over medium heat for 20 minutes or until golden brown, turning occasionally. Drain on paper towels. Yields 2 servings.

Eurcle Culipher, Jackson North Council (Book 2)

Mississippi Fried Chicken

6 chicken breast halves
Salt and pepper to taste
1 cup flour
½ teaspoon salt

½ teaspoon black pepper
1 teaspoon baking powder
Cooking oil

In colander, rinse chicken breasts; salt and pepper. Let stand to drain. In plastic bag, combine flour, salt, pepper, and baking powder. Shake chicken in this mixture until well coated. Refrigerate 6 hours. Put 1 inch of cooking oil in skillet; heat to medium-high. Place chicken in skillet. When chicken pieces are hot and cooking well, reduce heat to medium-low. Cook 7–10 minutes on each side or until well browned.

Maurice Gole, Tupelo Council (Book 1)

Barbeque Chicken

Chicken, of your choice
3 tablespoons butter or
  drippings
1 large onion, finely chopped
½ cup chopped bell pepper
¼ cup finely chopped celery
  (optional)
1 cup water

½ cup sweet pickle juice
1 tablespoon vinegar or
  lemon juice
2 tablespoons Worcestershire
1 cup ketchup
1 tablespoon prepared mustard
2 tablespoons brown sugar
Salt and pepper to taste

Flour and brown chicken in skillet with butter. Transfer chicken to a baking dish and drain all drippings except 3 tablespoons. To drippings add onion, bell pepper, and celery, if desired; cook until tender. Add remaining ingredients and cook 15–20 minutes or to boiling point. Pour sauce over chicken and bake, covered, in 325° oven for about 45 minutes or until chicken is done.

Dot McAlpin, Jackson North Council (Book 2)

Detroit, Michigan, was the first city in the nation to assign individual telephone numbers in 1879.

Chicken Curry (Indian Style)

2 small onions, shredded
1 stick butter or margarine
¾ teaspoon red pepper
½ teaspoon cumin seed
⅛ teaspoon ground cloves
⅙ teaspoon ground ginger
⅛ teaspoon ground cinnamon

⅓ teaspoon turmeric
1 teaspoon salt
1 (6-ounce) can tomato sauce
1 (2-pound) chicken, cut up and skin removed
1½ cups water
½ teaspoon black pepper

Sauté onions in butter. Add spices, salt, and tomato sauce. Add chicken and cook for 40 minutes, turning every 10 minutes longer. Add water and cook 10 minutes longer. Add pepper and cook for 10 minutes. Serve over rice or slices of bread.

Mrs. K. K. Chawla, Greenwood Council (Book 1)

Lemon Chicken

SAUCE:
1 tablespoon soy sauce
½ teaspoon salt
½ teaspoon pepper
⅓ cup salad oil

½ cup lemon juice
2 tablespoons grated lemon rind
1 clove garlic, crushed

Mix all ingredients for Sauce, and refrigerate until ready to use.

½ cup flour
1 teaspoon salt
½ teaspoon pepper

2 teaspoons paprika
1 (3- to 3½-pound) chicken
½ cup butter, melted

Mix flour and seasonings in paper sack. Drop in chicken and shake to coat well. Melt butter in baking pan and place chicken, skin side down. Bake at 400º for 30 minutes. Pour Sauce over chicken. Cook for 30 more minutes or until done.

Anna Earls, Greenwood Council (Book 3)

Ten Minute Chicken

1 (4-ounce) can sliced
  mushrooms
1 (10¾-ounce) can cream of
  mushroom soup
½ cup milk
¾ teaspoon seasoned salt

2 (5-ounce) cans boned chicken,
  drained
¼ teaspoon salt
⅛ teaspoon pepper
Cooked rice

Place all ingredients, except rice, in a saucepan. Stir and cook for 10 minutes. Serve over cooked rice.

Sue Hatten (Book 3)

Chicken Dinner in a Skillet

2 whole chicken breasts, split
2 tablespoons butter or
  margarine
2 medium potatoes, peeled
  and quartered
2 stalks celery, cut into 2-inch
  slices

½ cup sliced carrots
1 bay leaf
¼ teaspoon poultry seasoning
¼ cup water
1 (10¾-ounce) can Cheddar
  cheese soup, undiluted

Brown chicken on both sides in butter; add remaining ingredients to skillet. Bring to a boil; cover and simmer 30 minutes, stirring occasionally. Remove bay leaf. For 2 servings, serve 2 chicken pieces and half the sauce immediately.

Note: To freeze remainder, line a 1-quart casserole with aluminum foil, spoon remaining mixture into prepared dish, wrap foil securely around mixture, and place in freezer. After mixture is frozen, remove from dish and return wrapped portion to freezer.

Eurcle Culipher, Jackson North Council (Book 2)

Chicken Pilau

¾ stick margarine
1 (10¾-ounce) can onion soup
1 (10¾-ounce) can cream of
  chicken soup
2 cans water

½ cup uncooked rice
1 medium green bell pepper
1 large fryer
1 tablespoon salt
½–1 teaspoon red pepper

Melt margarine in shallow roasting pan. Add soups, water, rice, and bell pepper. Cut fryer into serving pieces and season to taste. Place chicken in pan and cover with foil. Bake in oven at 350º for 1 hour; remove foil and let cook, uncovered, until golden brown.

Frances W. Caffey (Book 3)

Chicken and Drop Dumplings

1 stewing chicken, cut up
3 teaspoons salt, divided
½ teaspoon black pepper,
  divided

1½ cups sifted all-purpose flour
2 teaspoons baking powder
4 teaspoons shortening
¾ cup milk

Place cut chicken in large stockpot; add 2 teaspoons salt and ¼ teaspoon pepper and cover with water. Put lid on pot and simmer gently until tender. Allow to cool, then debone. Return meat to broth.

Sift together flour, baking powder, and remaining salt and pepper. Cut in shortening with a pastry blender until the mixture resembles cornmeal. Add milk and stir only enough to mix well. Drop by tablespoons onto stewed chicken in boiling broth. Cook 10 minutes covered, and 10 more minutes uncovered.

Lynn Rackley, Capitol Life Member Club (Book 1)

Mushroom Chicken with Drop Dumplings

1 fryer, cut up, or chicken
  breasts, cut in strips
2 tablespoons oil
2 (10¾-ounce) cans cream of
  mushroom soup
1 large onion, chopped
Salt and pepper to taste
Garlic powder to taste
1 cup water

Brown chicken in hot oil; drain. Put browned chicken in heavy pot with lid. Add 1 cup water, soup, onion, salt and pepper, and garlic powder. Cover and cook 50–55 minutes or until chicken is cooked. Keep plenty of gravy on chicken.

DROP DUMPLINGS:

1½ cups self-rising flour
1 egg
⅔ cup milk
1 tablespoon shortening,
  melted, or oil

Add flour to egg, milk, and oil mixture. When chicken is done, drop dumplings into hot gravy. Cover and cook 8–10 minutes, until done.

Ott Brockman, Hattiesburg, MS (Book 4)

Chicken Baked in Sour Cream

2–2½ pounds boneless,
skinless chicken breasts
2 teaspoons Ac'cent, divided
4 tablespoons butter or
margarine
1 small onion, finely chopped
3 tablespoons flour
1 cup water

1 cup sour cream
1 teaspoon paprika
½ teaspoon grated lemon rind
1 teaspoon salt
½ teaspoon black pepper
2 tablespoons cooking sherry
2 tablespoons chopped fresh
parsley

Wash and dry chicken breasts thoroughly. Sprinkle chicken on all sides with 1½ teaspoons Ac'cent. Let stand about 15 minutes.

Melt butter in a heavy skillet over moderate heat. Add chicken and brown slowly on all sides. Remove chicken and place in a 2-quart casserole dish; set aside.

Sauté onion in same pan in remainder of butter over low heat until tender. Stir in flour, water, and sour cream. Cook, stirring constantly until thickened. Add paprika, lemon rind, salt, pepper, and remaining Ac'cent. Blend and pour over chicken. Cover and bake for 1 hour at 350º. Add sherry and parsley. Blend and serve over hot rice.

Carolyn Stafford, Hattiesburg Council (Book 2)

Chicken Enchilada Casserole

1 (2½- to 3-pound) chicken
½ cup finely chopped onion
1 (10¾-ounce) can cream of
mushroom soup
1 (10¾-ounce) can cream of
chicken soup
1 (4-ounce) can chopped green
chiles

¼ teaspoon pepper
Salt to taste
1 (10-ounce) can chicken broth*
12 tortillas (corn or flour)
1 (8-ounce) package sharp
shredded Cheddar cheese

Cook and debone chicken; cut into bite-size pieces. Sauté onion in a little butter. Add soups, green chiles, pepper, salt, and broth; blend well and heat until thickened. Heat tortillas in a greased skillet just long enough to soften on both sides. Cover bottom of a greased 2½- or 3-quart casserole dish with 6 tortillas. Spread half the chicken over tortillas, then ½ the sauce, and ½ the cheese. Repeat process, ending with cheese. Bake at 350º for 35–30 minutes.

*If boiling chicken, use 1 cup reserved chicken broth instead of canned.

Ida Lee Barron, Jackson North Council (Book 1)

The coin-operated pay telephone was patented by William Gray of Hartford, Connecticut, in 1889.

Chicken and Spaghetti

1 hen
1 (16-ounce) package spaghetti
1 onion, chopped
2 tablespoons butter
1 (14½-ounce) can tomatoes
Salt and pepper to taste

3 teaspoons flour
¼ cup chicken broth
1 teaspoon Worcestershire
Butter for top
¾ pound grated Cheddar cheese

Cook hen; debone and cut into small pieces. Cook spaghetti; rinse. Sauté onion in butter until brown. Add tomatoes and season to taste. Mix flour with broth and add to sauce; simmer for 30 minutes. Mix sauce, chicken, and spaghetti. Dot with butter and then bake for 1 hour at 350º. Sprinkle top with cheese before serving.

Frances Caffey (Book 3)

Dorito Chicken Casserole

1 whole chicken fryer
1 large bag Nacho Doritos
Cheese, grated, divided
1 small onion, finely chopped
1 (11-ounce) can whole-kernel
   corn, drained

1 (10¾-ounce) cream of
   chicken soup
1 (10¾-ounce) cream of
   mushroom soup
1 cup milk
1 (10-ounce) can Ro-Tel tomatoes

Boil, debone, and cut up chicken. Layer chicken, Doritos, ½ the cheese, onion, and corn in casserole dish. Mix soups, milk, and tomatoes; pour over top and sprinkle with remaining cheese. Bake at 375º for about 30 minutes.

Shirley Clanton, Natchez Council (Book 1)

Chicken Ro-Tel Casserole

2 large chickens
1 (10-ounce) can chicken broth
2 large onions, chopped
2 large bell peppers, chopped
1 (7-ounce) package vermicelli
1 (10-ounce) can Ro-Tel
   tomatoes, mashed

2 tablespoons Worcestershire
1 cup tiny green peas, drained
1 (8-ounce) can sliced
   mushrooms, drained
1 (16-ounce) box Velveeta
1 stick margarine

Boil chicken and save at least 1½ quarts of broth (if not enough broth, add chicken broth with water to make 1½ quarts). Cool, debone, and cut in chunks.

Sauté onions and bell peppers. Cook vermicelli in reserved broth; don't drain. Add tomatoes and Worcestershire; cook 5 more minutes. Add sautéed onions and peppers, peas, and mushrooms. Add cheese, cut in chunks, and stir over low heat until cheese is melted. Add chicken; stir thoroughly. Cook 45 minutes at 350º. If you freeze it, let thaw before cooking.

Ida Lee Barron, Jackson North Council and Eleanor Well,
Greenwood Council (Book 1)

Chicken Casserole

2 cups cooked, chopped
   chicken
1 (8-ounce) carton sour cream
1 (10¾-ounce) can cream of
   chicken soup
½ cup milk

Chopped onion
Salt and pepper to taste
Cheese crackers or Ritz
   Crackers, crushed
Poppy seeds

Mix all ingredients together, except crackers and poppy seeds. Place in casserole dish. Sprinkle top with cracker crumbs and poppy seeds. Bake at 350º for 30 minutes or until it bubbles. Good with a buttered, parsley rice.

Carol Sparks, Meridian Council (Book 1)

Chicken, Broccoli and Rice Casserole

½ stick butter
⅓ cup chopped onion
½ cup chopped celery
1 (10-ounce) package frozen, chopped broccoli
1 (10¾-ounce) can cream of mushroom soup

1 cup uncooked instant rice
1 soup can milk
2 tablespoons sugar
1 (8-ounce) jar Cheez Whiz
1 cup cooked, cubed chicken
1 tablespoon chopped pimento

Melt butter; add onion and celery. Let simmer while preparing remaining ingredients. Drop broccoli in boiling, salted water long enough to separate (do not cook); drain. Mix soup, rice, milk, sugar, Cheez Whiz, broccoli, chicken, and pimento in a large bowl. Add celery and onions. Pour into a 6½x9-inch buttered Pyrex dish. Cook 40 minutes, covered, at 350º. Uncover and cook another 10–15 minutes until bubbly in the middle.

Hint: Serve as a main dish, or omit chicken for a side dish. Can substitute shrimp or crab for chicken.

Teresa Sheilds, Jackson South Council (Book 2)

Party Chicken Casserole

4½ whole chicken breasts,
cooked, deboned
1 (8-ounce) can sliced water
chestnuts
2 (10¾-ounce) cans cream of
mushroom soup
1 cup mayonnaise
1 pimiento, chopped
¾ cup finely chopped celery
¾ cup finely chopped onion
½ teaspoon poultry seasoning
Salt and pepper to taste
Lemon pepper seasoning to taste
½ package Pepperidge Farm
stuffing mix
½ cup chicken broth

Mix all ingredients, except stuffing mix and broth, together and fill a 3-quart casserole. Top with stuffing mix and moisten with broth. Can be fixed the day before. Bake at 350°, uncovered, 40–50 minutes. Serves 8–10.

Mrs. John Levasseur, Meridian Council (Book 1)

Chicken Pot Pie

4 or 5 chicken breasts, cooked
and cut into bite-size pieces
4 hard-boiled eggs, sliced
1½ cups chicken broth
1 (10¾-ounce) can cream of
chicken soup
1 (17-ounce) can mixed
vegetables
1 stick margarine
1 cup self-rising flour
1 cup milk
Salt and pepper to taste

Place chicken in casserole dish; layer eggs over chicken. Mix broth with soup and vegetables; pour over chicken and eggs. Melt margarine and mix with flour and milk. Pour this over top of casserole. Season to taste. Bake at 350° until crust is brown, about 30 minutes. Batter will make its own beautiful crust.

Gayle Hall, Tupelo Club, Baldwyn, MS (Book 4)

Easy Chicken Pie

4–6 chicken breasts, or 1 large
  fryer
1 (12- or 16-ounce) package
  noodles

½ cup sweet milk
Salt and pepper to taste
1 stick pie crust*
Butter or margarine (optional)

Boil chicken until done; reserve broth. Remove chicken and set aside to cool. Add enough water to broth to make 4–6 cups liquid; bring to a boil. Add noodles. Cook until tender, adding milk (a little more or less won't usually matter) in 2 or 3 parts as the noodles cook; salt and pepper to taste. Do not overcook. Place in large casserole baking dish. Add deboned chicken. Cover with crust; prick holes in top. Make design in crust if you so choose. Dot with butter or margarine, if desired. Bake about 45 minutes in 350º oven or until golden brown and bubbly. Serves 8–10 people amply. May be made ahead and frozen.

*Can be found in the refrigerator section and usually comes 2 to a pack.

Note: I add about ½ small onion and about ¼ cup chopped celery to my chicken when cooking; enhances the flavor of the chicken pie.

Edwena Lowther, Jackson South Council (Book 1)

Easy Chicken Pie

1 chicken, boiled and deboned
3 hard-boiled eggs, sliced
1½ cups chicken broth
1 (10¾-ounce) can cream of
  chicken soup

1 stick butter or margarine,
  melted
1 cup self-rising flour
1 cup milk

In a large, buttered casserole dish, layer chicken and sliced eggs. Mix broth and chicken soup; pour over chicken and eggs. Mix butter and flour well; mix with milk. Pour over chicken and soup. Cook for 1½ hours at 325º.

Eloise Stephenson, Meridian Life Member Club (Book 2)

Chicken Supreme

4 chicken breasts
1½ cups water
½ cup chopped onion
½ cup chopped green bell
  pepper
½ cup chopped celery
2 tablespoons butter
1 (10¾-ounce) can cream of
  chicken soup

1 (10¾-ounce) can cream of
  celery soup
1 cup chicken broth (reserved
  from boiling chicken)
1 (8-ounce) package spaghetti
Paprika
Parsley
Salt and pepper to taste

Boil chicken breasts in water about 30 minutes; reserve broth. Set breasts aside to cool. After they have cooled, cut into 1-inch, bite-size squares. Sauté onion, bell pepper, and celery in butter until slightly tender. Mix sautéed vegetables, chicken, soups, and 1 cup reserved broth. Cook spaghetti as directed. Combine chicken-soup mixture with spaghetti in greased casserole dish. Sprinkle with paprika, parsley, and salt and pepper to taste. Cover with foil to keep spaghetti from drying out. Bake at 325° for 30 minutes.

A. J. Stanovich, Gulf Coast Council (Book 2)

Chicken Squares

1 (3-ounce) package cream
  cheese, softened
3 tablespoons margarine,
  melted, divided
2 cups cooked, cubed chicken
¼ teaspoon salt
⅛ teaspoon pepper

2 tablespoons milk
1 tablespoon chopped onion
1 tablespoon chopped pimiento
1 (8-ounce) can crescent dinner
  rolls
¾ cup crushed seasoned
  croutons

In medium bowl, blend cream cheese and 2 tablespoons margarine until smooth. Add next 6 ingredients; mix well. Separate crescent dough into 4 rectangles; firmly press perforations to seal. Spoon ½ cup meat mixture into center of each rectangle. Pull 4 corners of dough to top center of chicken mixture; twist slightly and seal edges. Brush tops with remaining tablespoon margarine; dip in crouton crumbs. Place on ungreased cookie sheet and bake at 350° for 20–25 minutes until golden brown.

Mrs. Etta R. Tawam, Jackson North Council (Book 1)

Chicken Bites

6–8 chicken breasts
1½ cups buttermilk
1 package ranch dressing mix
  (original)

2 cups flour
1 teaspoon turmeric
Salt and pepper to taste

Debone chicken breasts and cut into bite-size pieces. Marinate overnight in buttermilk and ranch dressing mix.

Dip in flour seasoned with turmeric, salt and pepper; fry in hot oil until golden brown. Drain. Can be frozen and reheated.

Teresa Shields, Jackson South Council (Book 1)

Chicken Delight

LAYER 1:

1 (8-ounce) package Stove Top
  seasoned cornbread stuffing
  mix

1 stick margarine, melted
1 cup water

Mix lightly. Put ½ mixture in 8x12-inch casserole dish.

LAYER 2:

2½ cups chopped, cooked
  chicken
½ cup chopped celery

½ cup chopped onion
½ cup mayonnaise
¾ teaspoon salt

Mix ingredients, and pour over Layer 1 in casserole.

LAYER 3:

2 eggs
1½ cups milk

1 (10¾-ounce) can cream of
  mushroom soup

Beat eggs; add 1½ cups milk and pour over Layer 2 in casserole.
Add remaining ½ bread mixture. Cover with foil and refrigerate
overnight.

Take out 1 hour before baking and spread mushroom soup on
top. Bake uncovered in 325° oven for 45 minutes.

Louie Elizabeth Dodds, Jackson North Council (Book 1)

Chicken or Turkey
with Dressing and Gravy

CORNBREAD:

2 cups self-rising cornmeal
  mix
1 egg, beaten

1 tablespoon oil
1⅓ cups buttermilk
1 tablespoon sugar (optional)

Grease 9-inch pan or skillet; heat skillet in oven while it is preheating to 450°. Combine all ingredients. Mix well and pour into hot pan. Bake 20–25 minutes, until golden brown on top.

DRESSING:

1 (4- to 6-pound) hen or turkey
Skillet of Cornbread
5 slices toasted bread
5 biscuits
5 green onions, chopped fine
  (tops included)
1 large onion, chopped fine

5 ribs celery, chopped fine
1 boiled egg, chopped
1¼ quarts chicken broth,
  cooled to room temperature
3 raw eggs, beaten
Salt and pepper to taste

Cook chicken or turkey until tender; reserve broth. Crumble Cornbread, bread, and biscuits; cool. Add chopped green onions, onion, and celery. Add boiled egg. Pour chicken broth, beaten eggs, salt and pepper over mixture. Mix well. Be sure the mixture is soupy.

Pour into greased 9x13x2-inch baking dish. Bake at 350° for 1 hour or until top is golden brown. Serve with meat and Gravy.

GRAVY:

1 quart chicken broth
Chicken giblets, chopped
1 boiled egg, chopped

4 tablespoons plain flour mixed
  with water until smooth
Salt and pepper to taste

Heat broth; add giblets and egg. Pour flour mixture in, stirring constantly to keep from lumping. Cook until desired thickness. Season to taste.

Beth Harbour, Meridian, MS (Book 4)

Deep-Fried Turkey

MARINADE:

6 tablespoons Tony Chachere's seasoning
3 tablespoons Chef Paul's poultry seasoning
1 tablespoon red pepper

1 teaspoon garlic powder
2 teaspoons Ac'cent seasoning
4½ cups water
½ stick butter

Bring all ingredients, except butter, to a boil while stirring constantly. Let cool for about an hour, allowing water to absorb the seasonings. Boil and stir once more. Strain (a tea strainer works fine) to remove the large pieces of seasoning (to keep the meat injector needle from stopping up). Melt butter in the seasoned water. When cool enough to put in the needle, you are ready to inject the turkey.

1 (10- to 12-pound) turkey   4–8 gallons peanut oil

Inject Marinade at different depths throughout the turkey. Season inside and outside with additional Chachere's and Chef Paul's seasoning. Place in deep roasting pan and refrigerate overnight.

In a pot large enough to hold a whole turkey, pour peanut oil to fill half full. Bring oil to 350° and insert turkey for 5 minutes using a wire basket, or wire through the cavity to make handles so that the turkey may be lifted out of the oil. Cook between 300° and 325° for 4 minutes per pound. Do not cook indoors as oil tends to splatter.

Gus Pique, Jr. (Book 3)

Turkey Creole

1 (2-pound) turkey
½ cup chopped onion
½ cup chopped bell pepper
1 clove garlic, minced
¾ cup uncooked rice
1 (16-ounce) can diced
  tomatoes, reserve juice
2 slices bacon, cooked and
  crumbled

½ teaspoon salt
¼ teaspoon red pepper sauce
2½ cups chicken broth or water
10 ounces fresh okra, washed,
  cut up
⅛ teaspoon black pepper

Bake turkey. (Armour brand turkey roast in a foil pan is easy and good to use.) Cool, debone, and chop.

Sauté onion, bell pepper, and garlic until tender. Add rice, stirring to coat. Add tomatoes, bacon, salt, pepper sauce, and chopped turkey. Combine broth and reserved tomato juice with onion mixture; stir in okra and black pepper. Cover and simmer for about 15 minutes or until rice is tender.

Pat Munn, Jackson South Council (Book 2)

$\mathcal{S}$eafood

1959
Princess

The desk set received a smart, new look. Compactness, attractive styling and illuminated dial (it lights up when you lift the handset or you can keep it on as a night light) contributed to the all-around usefulness of the Princess set. Featured in a variety or colors, including pastels, its design appealed to women and teenage girls. The Princess was unique in two aspects: it required an external electric transformer to power the light-up dial, and when production began it did not contain enough room for a bell ringer, so an external ringer was required. The Princess model remained in production until 1994 with several modifications throughout the years.

With the first transcontinental microwave transmitting system now in operation, true number calling is instituted—that is, seven numerical digits without letters or names—although it took more than fifteen years to implement throughout the system. But cables provide much higher signal quality, avoid atmospheric interference, and offer greater capacity and security.

Stuffed Crabs
or Filling for Crab Po-Boys

1 bell pepper, chopped
1 stalk celery with leaves,
 chopped
½ stick margarine or ⅓ cup
 olive oil
1 large onion, chopped
1 bunch green onions, tops
 included, finely chopped
¼ teaspoon liquid crab boil
Salt and black pepper to taste

Louisiana hot sauce to taste
1 tablespoon dried parsley,
 or ¼ cup chopped fresh
 parsley
6 cloves garlic, minced
3 cups French bread crumbs
 for stuffed crabs (or 1 cup
 dried crumbs for po-boys)
1 pound cooked crabmeat

Cook bell pepper and celery in margarine or oil until celery starts to soften. Add onion and green onions and cook until onions are clear, not brown. Add 1 cup water and simmer for a few minutes. (For po-boys, add only ½ cup of water). Add remaining ingredients and mix well.

For Stuffed Crabs: Pile in buttered, clean crab shells or individual casseroles. Put a pat of margarine on top of each and bake for about 20 minutes at 350º.

For Crab Po-Boys: Continue to cook on top of stove until slightly dry, then serve hot on French bread with mayonnaise or butter, lettuce, and tomato.

A. J. Stanovich, Gulf Coast Council (Book 2)

Crabmeat au Gratin

1 celery stalk, finely chopped
1 cup finely chopped onion
1 stick margarine
½ cup all-purpose flour
1½ (12-ounce) cans
  evaporated milk
2 egg yolks, beaten
1 teaspoon salt
½ teaspoon red pepper
¼ teaspoon black pepper
1 pound white crabmeat
1 (8-ounce) jar Cheez Whiz

Sauté celery and onion in margarine until onions are wilted. Blend flour in well with this mixture. Pour in the milk gradually, stirring constantly. Add egg yolks, salt, and peppers. Cook for 5 minutes. Put crabmeat in bowl suitable for mixing, and pour the sauce over crabmeat. Blend well and transfer into a lightly greased casserole dish. Add Cheez Whiz to top and bake at 375º for 10–15 minutes or until lightly browned. Serves 6.

Note: This may be divided into 6 individual ramekins, and frozen.

Betty Robb, Jackson South Council (Book 2)

Baked Oysters Bienville

Rock salt
2 teaspoons margarine
2 cloves garlic, minced
¼ cup sliced green onions
¼ cup chopped parsley
¼ teaspoon hot sauce
¼ cup soft bread crumbs
¼ cup grated Parmesan cheese
⅛ teaspoon ground black pepper
1 dozen oysters on the half shell
Juice of 1 lemon

Sprinkle a thin layer of rock salt in a shallow pan; set aside. Coat a skillet with cooking spray and place over medium to high heat until hot. Add margarine, garlic, onions, and parsley; sauté until onions are tender. Add hot sauce, bread crumbs, Parmesan, and pepper; stir. Spoon mixture evenly onto oysters. Bake at 425º for 6–8 minutes or until edges of oysters begin to curl. Squeeze lemon juice over oysters before serving over rock salt.

Angela L. McCoy, Jackson Council (Book 3)

Tuna Puffs

1⅓ cups potato flakes
⅔ cup powdered milk (dry)
1½ cups boiling water
2 tablespoons plus 2 teaspoons butter or margarine
½ cup chopped onion
2 egg whites, lightly beaten
1 (8-ounce) can solid white albacore tuna, drained
Dash of garlic salt
Dash of black pepper

Mix potato flakes and powdered milk. Add water and butter, mixing well. Add remaining ingredients and mix. Form mixture into 12 equal mounds on nonstick baking sheet. Bake for 12–18 minutes at 350º until they start to brown. Serves 4.

Chris Watts, Greenwood Council (Book 3)

Mother's Jambalaya

1 tablespoon oil	1 bell pepper, chopped
1 tablespoon flour	1 tablespoon minced parsley
1 (16-ounce) package cooked,	1 teaspoon Worcestershire
chopped ham	Salt, pepper, and paprika to taste
1 (14-ounce) can diced tomatoes	4 cups water
1 medium onion, chopped	1 cup uncooked rice
1 clove garlic, crushed	1 cup shrimp, peeled, deveined

Mix oil and flour over low heat; stir until smooth and light brown. Add ham, and tomatoes; cook for 3–5 minutes. Add onion, garlic, bell pepper, seasonings, and water. Simmer about 10 minutes and add rice; bring to a boil, then simmer about 30 minutes until rice is tender. Keep covered while cooking. Do not stir during this time, but keep it on low and watch carefully so as not to burn. After rice is cooked, add shrimp, stir, and cook about 5 minutes, just until shrimp are pink and curled.

Lynn Ainsworth, Jackson South Council (Book 2)

In the early days, operators working at a large switchboard would answer an incoming telephone call and connect it manually to the party being called. The first automatic telephone exchange was patented by Almon Strowger of Kansas City in 1891 and installed in 1892, but manual switchboards remained in common use. The last manual switchboard in the Southern Bell region was removed from service in Rosedale, Mississippi, on September 21, 1969.

Spanish-Style Shrimp and Rice

3 tablespoons olive oil
1 medium onion, chopped
1 clove garlic, crushed
½ cup chopped celery
¼ cup chopped bell pepper
½ cup long-grain rice
1 (16-ounce) can tomatoes,
   undrained

1½ cups water
¼ teaspoon pepper
1½ teaspoons salt
½ teaspoon oregano
1 teaspoon ground coriander
1 (7½-ounce) can shrimp
2 pimientos, cut up
½ cup grated Cheddar cheese

In a deep 10-inch skillet, heat oil; add onion, garlic, celery, and bell pepper. Cook gently, stirring often, until tender but not brown. Add rice, tomatoes (including juice), water, salt, pepper, oregano, and coriander. Simmer about 20 minutes or until rice is tender and most of the liquid is absorbed. Drain shrimp, adding liquid to rice mixture. Add to rice mixture with pimiento. Bring to simmer (just to heat shrimp through). Spoon into 4 (1¼-cup) individual baking dishes. Sprinkle with grated cheese; heat under broiler long enough to melt cheese, 2–3 minutes. Serve at once. Makes 4 main-dish servings.

Kent Holden, Jackson North Council (Book 1)

Pioneer Shrimp Boil Shrimp Sauce

This is the best shrimp sauce in the world and believe it or not, we have to make more than ten gallons for our shrimp boil every year. This recipe was submitted in loving memory of Pat Jones, who, ever since I can remember, has cooked our shrimp. How we are going to miss him.

½ stalk celery, chopped
½ bell pepper, chopped
1 onion, chopped
½ box garlic, peeled, chopped
4 cups mayonnaise
½ cup mustard
Scant ½ cup salt
¼ cup Lea & Perrins sauce
1½ cups lemon juice
½ tablespoon Tabasco
1½ tablespoons black pepper
1 teaspoon paprika
½ cup horseradish
2 cups ketchup
1½ cups Wesson oil
1½ (10-ounce) bottles chili
   sauce

Combine celery, bell pepper, onions, and garlic; add all other ingredients and mix well. Put entire mixture through blender. Makes ½ gallon.

FOR TEN GALLONS:
7 stalks celery
8 bell peppers
16 onions
6 boxes garlic
6 gallons mayonnaise
12 (6-ounce) bottles mustard
2 (26-ounce) boxes salt
2 (15-ounce) bottles Lea &
   Perrins sauce
10 (16-ounce) bottles lemon juice
2 (2-ounce) bottles Tabasco
2 (6-ounce) boxes black pepper
2 (1.62-ounce) paprika
6 (8-ounce) jars horseradish
10 (14-ounce) bottles ketchup
1½ gallons Wesson oil
20 (10-ounce) bottles chili
   sauce

Prepare as for ½ gallon.

Lou Sparks, Jackson South Council (Book 1)

Quick Shrimp Curry

½ cup chopped onion
1 tablespoon butter or
  margarine
1 (10-ounce) can condensed
  cream of shrimp soup
1 cup sour cream
½ teaspoon curry powder
1 cup shrimp, fresh or canned

3 cups cooked rice
Paprika and fresh parsley
  for garnish
Condiments: salted peanuts,
  chopped hard-boiled eggs,
  chutney, and kumquat
  preserves

Cook onion in butter until tender. Add soup; heat and stir until smooth. Stir in sour cream and curry powder. Add shrimp and cook over medium heat until done. Serve over hot rice; sprinkle with paprika and add sprig of parsley. Offer curry condiments such as salted peanuts, chopped hard-boiled eggs, chutney, and kumquat preserves. Serves 4.

Lula Cade, Capitol Life Member (Book 2)

Marinated Shrimp

Great as an appetizer, first course, or main dish salad.

5 pounds raw shrimp in shells,
  cooked and cleaned
1 cup vegetable oil
½ cup vinegar
1¼ cups finely chopped celery
2½ tablespoons finely
  chopped green pepper
4 tablespoons grated onion

1 clove garlic, chopped fine
5 tablespoons chopped fresh
  parsley
¾ cup horseradish mustard
1½ teaspoons salt
¼ teaspoon pepper
4 tablespoons paprika

Place shrimp in large deep bowl. Combine remaining ingredients thoroughly and pour over shrimp. Cover and marinate in refrigerator for 24 hours before serving, stirring occasionally. Yields 10–12 servings.

Jane Sisson (Book 3)

Barbequed Shrimp

5 pounds fresh shrimp,
   unpeeled
3–4 cloves garlic, minced
1 bunch celery with leaves,
   very coarsely chopped
6 lemons, cut in halves

4 sticks butter, cut into cubes
½–1 (2¼-ounce) jar cracked
   black pepper
Worcestershire to taste
1–2 tablespoons salt
Hot sauce to taste

Wash shrimp thoroughly and place in a very large, shallow pan. Add garlic and celery. Squeeze lemon juice over the top of shrimp and reserve. Dot shrimp with butter and sprinkle with remaining seasonings. Arrange lemon halves on top. Place shrimp under broiler until butter melts, and the shrimp starts to turn pink; about 5 minutes, stirring. When all shrimp are slightly pink, reduce temperature to 350º and bake for 20 minutes or until done, stirring often. Do not overcook or shrimp will become mushy. Serve hot with plenty of French bread to dip in the juice. Yields 4 large servings.

Laverne Brantley, Telco (Book 2)

Shrimp au Jus

3 pounds shrimp, unpeeled
1 teaspoon cracked red pepper
½ teaspoon black pepper
½ teaspoon garlic powder
3 sticks butter
⅓ cup soy sauce

⅓ cup Worcestershire
Juice of 1 lemon
3 leaves fresh sweet basil
   (optional)
2 teaspoons salt

Wash shrimp well and place in a glass casserole dish or baking dish. Sprinkle with peppers and garlic. Combine butter, soy sauce, Worcestershire, lemon, and basil leaves in a large glass measuring cup; heat in microwave on HIGH 1½–2 minutes. Pour over shrimp and seal top of casserole dish with plastic wrap. Cook shrimp in casserole with microwave oven set on HIGH for 10–12 minutes, stirring once or twice during cooking. Remove from heat and sprinkle with salt. Serve hot with French bread for dipping in sauce.

Charles J. LeBlanc, Jackson Council (Book 3)

Flounder Crabmeat Roll-Up

4 large flounder fillets
Seasoned salt to taste
Black pepper to taste
1 cup crabmeat

1 (10¾-ounce) can light cream
   of mushroom soup
Paprika

Sprinkle fillets with seasoned salt and black pepper. Top each fillet with ¼ cup crabmeat. Roll up and place in a greased oblong casserole dish. Pour mushroom soup over fillets. Cover and bake at 350º for about 30 minutes or until fish flakes. Remove cover and sprinkle with paprika. Cook for another 5 minutes.

Note: This is also good made with catfish fillets.

Charlene Porter, Life Member, Natchez Council (Book 3)

Oven-Fried Fish Fillets

1 pound sole or flounder fillets
¼ cup mayonnaise
Bread crumbs
Paprika
½ teaspoon salt
¼ teaspoon pepper
Lemon wedges

Thinly coat fish fillets with mayonnaise; dredge each in bread crumbs. Arrange in a greased 9x13-inch baking pan; sprinkle fillets with seasonings. Bake at 450° for about 12 minutes or until fish flakes easily when tested with a fork. Garnish fillets with lemon wedges. Yields 2 servings.

Eurcle Culipher, Jackson North Council (Book 2)

Baked Fish

4 stems celery, including tops, chopped
½ small bunch parsley, chopped, or 2 tablespoons dried parsley flakes
1 cup chopped green onions
2 tablespoons olive oil or Wesson oil
1 (8-ounce) can tomato sauce
1 (16-ounce) can tomatoes, drained
1 tablespoon dried oregano leaves
1 teaspoon garlic powder
1 medium-size red snapper or flounder
Lemon juice (optional)

In skillet over low heat, add all chopped vegetables to oil and cook until tender; add tomato sauce, tomatoes, oregano, and garlic powder. Mix well. Place fish in 9x13-inch baking dish and pour mixed ingredients over fish. Cover with foil and bake at 300° for 1 hour. Serve with lemon juice, if desired.

Variation: Chicken is very good prepared this way and may be substituted for fish, either cut up or in halves.

Mrs. Carl Rayfield, Greenwood Council (Book 2)

Wrapped Farm-Raised Catfish with Cream Cheese Stuffing

4 (6- to 8-ounce) farm-raised
  catfish fillets, fresh or frozen
1 teaspoon salt, divided
½ teaspoon pepper, divided
1 tablespoon plus 1 teaspoon
  lemon juice, divided
1 cup fresh bread crumbs
3 tablespoons cream cheese,
  softened

1 tablespoon chopped celery
1 tablespoon chopped onion
1 teaspoon dehydrated parsley
  flakes
1 teaspoon ground thyme
8 slices bacon
Lemon slices
Pimiento strips

Thaw fish, if frozen. Season with ½ teaspoon salt and ¼ teaspoon pepper. Sprinkle fish with 1 teaspoon lemon juice. Combine bread crumbs, cream cheese, remaining 1 tablespoon lemon juice, celery, onion, parsley, thyme, remaining ½ teaspoon salt, and remaining ¼ teaspoon pepper. Divide stuffing into 4 portions. Place 1 portion of stuffing at one end of each fillet of fish. Roll fish around stuffing. Fry bacon until cooked, but not crisp. Wrap 2 slices bacon around each fillet; secure with a toothpick. Place fish rolls in a lightly greased baking dish. Bake in 350° oven for 15–20 minutes or until fish flakes easily when tested with a fork. Garnish with lemon slices and pimiento strips. Makes 4 servings.

Note: Remove toothpicks before serving.

Doris Kelly, Jackson North Council (Book 2)

Baked Catfish

¼ cup yellow cornmeal
¼ cup all-purpose flour
¼ cup grated Parmesan cheese
1 teaspoon paprika
½ teaspoon salt
½ teaspoon black pepper

1 egg
2 tablespoons milk
4 (4-ounce) catfish fillets
½ teaspoon sesame seeds
   (optional)
Lemon wedges for garnish

Combine first 6 ingredients; set aside. Beat egg and milk together. Dip fillets in egg mixture and dredge in cornmeal mixture. Place on baking sheet coated with butter-flavored cooking spray. Sprinkle with sesame seeds, if desired. Bake at 350º for 30 minutes. Serve with lemon wedges.

Beth Harbour, Meridian, MS (Book 4)

Catfish with Shrimp and Sherry Sauce

¼ cup butter
2 tablespoons grated onion
¼ cup cornstarch or flour
2 cups whole milk
½ pound shrimp, peeled and
   deveined
¼ teaspoon curry powder
¼ teaspoon garlic powder

¼ teaspoon tarragon
2 teaspoons Worcestershire
¼ teaspoon pepper sauce or
   cayenne pepper
⅛ teaspoon yellow food
   coloring
¾ cup dry sherry
6 catfish fillets, broiled

Melt butter over low heat. Add onion and sauté until clear. Add cornstarch or flour and mix to smooth consistency. Add milk, stirring constantly until thickened. Add shrimp, curry powder, garlic powder, tarragon, Worcestershire, pepper sauce, and food coloring. Cook over medium-low heat until shrimp are done, then add sherry. Serve over hot catfish fillets.

Charlene Porter (Book 3)

Farm-Raised Catfish Pizza

HUSH PUPPY CRUST:

1⅓ cups pie crust mix

⅔ cup hush puppy mix

4–5 tablespoons cold water

In a medium mixing bowl, combine pie crust mix and hush puppy mix. Add water gradually until mixture clings together and can be rolled into a ball. With fingertips, press dough into a lightly greased 12-inch pizza pan.

TARTAR TOPPING:

1 (10¾-ounce) can cream of onion soup

⅓ cup mayonnaise

¼ cup finely chopped dill pickles

2 tablespoons chopped pimento

Combine all ingredients; blend well.

1½ cups grated Cheddar or American cheese, divided

2 cups cooked, flaked, farm-raised catfish

¼ cup hush puppy mix

1½ teaspoons margarine, softened

Sprinkle half the cheese over the Hush Puppy Crust. Place the flaked fish on top of the cheese. Pour the Tartar Topping over the fish and sprinkle with remaining cheese. Combine hush puppy mix and margarine; sprinkle over top of cheese. Bake in a hot oven at 400° for 20–22 minutes. Serve hot. Serves 6.

Doris P. Kelly, Jackson North Council (Book 1)

Scalloped Salmon

1 (16-ounce) can salmon, bones
    removed, undrained
2 eggs
1 cup skim milk
1 onion, finely chopped
½ bell pepper, finely chopped
1 cup bread crumbs

Combine all ingredients and mix well. Spoon into a lightly greased 2-quart casserole dish. Bake for 1 hour in 350º oven or until firm and golden brown. Serves 6.

Charlene Porter, Life Member, Natchez Council (Book 3)

Salmon with Lime-Parsley Sauce

1 egg
1 clove garlic
1½ teaspoons fresh lime juice
½ teaspoon cumin
½ teaspoon salt
¼ teaspoon white pepper
½ cup vegetable or olive oil
⅓ cup chopped fresh parsley
2 fresh salmon fillets
Sliced almonds

Combine egg, garlic, lime juice, cumin, salt, and white pepper in a blender. Blend on low; pour in the oil in a fine stream while blending. Mixture should be very thick. Add chopped parsley and blend. (It will look like green mayo.) Place salmon in a baking dish. Top with sauce and sliced almonds. Bake at 350º for 8–10 minutes, just until the salmon is firm and starts to flake.

Vic Clark, Jackson, MS (Book 4)

Baked Red Snapper

1 (2½-pound) dressed red
  snapper, head and tail intact
2 cloves garlic, minced
1½ teaspoons peeled and
  minced ginger root
1 teaspoon reduced-sodium
  soy sauce

½ teaspoon white wine vinegar
1 teaspoon sesame oil
2 tablespoons minced fresh
  parsley

Make 3 deep diagonal slashes on both sides of snapper. Combine garlic, ginger root, soy sauce, vinegar, and oil in a bowl; rub mixture on inside and outside of snapper.

Place snapper in a 15½x10½x1-inch jellyroll pan coated with cooking spray. Cover tail loosely with aluminum foil and bake at 325° for 30–40 minutes, or until snapper flakes easily when tested with a fork. Transfer to a platter and garnish with parsley. Yields 8 servings.

Martha Alice Minyard, Tupelo Council-Future Pioneers (Book 3)

Cakes

1964
Touch-Tone

As America neared the 200 million mark in population, a new era in telephoning services began with push-button calling. Touch-Tone service was introduced, limiting errors and increasing the speed of dialing. A keypad replaced the familiar rotary "pulse" dial, and early Touch-Tone sets had only ten buttons. (The * and # keys were added in 1968.) The Touch-Tone system could travel across microwave transmitter links and work rapidly with solid state computer-controlled phone exchanges. A tone is produced as long as a key is depressed. No matter how long you press, the tone is decoded as the appropriate digit. The shortest duration in which a digit can be sent and decoded is about 100 milliseconds by automatic dialers. A twelve-digit long-distance phone number can be dialed by an automatic phone dialer in a little more than a second—about as long as it takes a pulse dial to send a single "0" digit.

Cream Cheese Pound Cake

2 sticks margarine, softened
1 stick butter, softened
1 (8-ounce) package cream
  cheese, softened
3 cups sugar

6 large eggs
3 cups sifted cake flour
1 teaspoon vanilla extract
1 teaspoon almond extract

Cream margarine, butter, and cream cheese together. Slowly add sugar and eggs, one at a time. Mix well and add flour, vanilla, and almond extract. Pour batter into greased and lightly floured Bundt pan. Place in cold oven. Bake 1½ hours at 285º. Do not open oven door while baking. Cool 20 minutes in pan after removing from oven. This is a moist cake that keeps well.

Billie Sue Rouse, Jackson North Council (Book 1)

Orange Pound Cake

1 (18¼-ounce) package butter
  cake mix
¾ cup oil
¾ cup milk
4 eggs, beaten

1 teaspoon orange extract
1 (3-ounce) package vanilla
  instant pudding mix
1 cup chopped pecans

Beat all ingredients together, except pecans. Grease tube pan. Sprinkle pecans around the bottom of the pan. Pour in batter and bake for 1 hour at 325º. Cool slightly and remove cake from pan.

TOPPING:
½ stick margarine
1½ cups confectioners' sugar

5 tablespoons fresh orange juice

Melt margarine in saucepan; stir in sugar and juice, and let come to a boil for a minute. Remove from heat; pour on cake while hot.

Patsy Tolleson, Jackson South Council (Book 2)

Five-Flavor Pound Cake

2 sticks butter or margarine,
  softened
½ cup Crisco shortening
3 cups sugar
5 eggs, well beaten
3 cups all-purpose flour or
  Swans Down Cake Flour

½ teaspoon baking powder
¾–1 cup milk
1 teaspoon coconut extract
1 teaspoon rum extract
1 teaspoon butter extract
1 teaspoon vanilla extract
1 teaspoon almond extract

Cream butter, shortening, and sugar until fluffy and light. Add eggs. Combine flour and baking powder; add to creamed mixture. Add milk alternately with flavorings. (If large eggs are used, only use ¾ cup milk.) Spoon into well-greased 10-inch tube pan. Bake at 300º–325º for 1½–2 hours. Glaze while hot.

GLAZE:

1 cup sugar
½ cup water
1 teaspoon coconut extract
1 teaspoon butter extract

1 teaspoon vanilla extract
1 teaspoon almond extract
1 teaspoon lemon extract

Mix in a heavy saucepan. Bring ingredients to a boil long enough to melt sugar. Have Glaze ready to pour when cake is removed from oven.

Lizzie D. Taylor, Columbus Club (Book 1)

Sour Cream Pound Cake

This has a crusty top.

3 cups all-purpose flour	6 eggs
¼ teaspoon baking soda	1 cup sour cream
2 sticks butter or margarine	1 teaspoon vanilla extract
3 cups sugar	

Sift flour and measure; resift twice with baking soda; set aside. Cream butter and add sugar slowly, beating constantly to cream well. Add eggs, one at a time, beating after each addition. Stir in sour cream. Add flour mixture ½ cup at a time, beating well. Stir in vanilla and turn batter into well-greased and floured 10-inch tube pan. Bake in 325º oven about 1½ hours or until cake is done.

Place pan on rack to cool 5 minutes. Loosen cake around edge of pan and edge of tube with dull side of knife. Press toward pan rather that toward cake; this protects crust. Turn cake onto rack to cool completely. Serve plain.

Note: One teaspoon lemon extract or ½ teaspoon almond flavoring may be used instead of vanilla.

Bessie Henley, Gulf Coast Council (Book 1)

Fresh Apple Cake

1½ cups salad oil
2 cups sugar
2 large eggs, beaten
2½ cups all-purpose flour
1 teaspoon salt
1 teaspoon baking soda

2 teaspoons baking powder
1 teaspoon vanilla extract
1 cup chopped pecans, mixed
  with a little flour
3 cups peeled, chopped raw
  apples

Beat salad oil and sugar at low speed until creamy; add eggs. Sift flour, salt, baking soda, and baking powder; add to egg mixture. Add vanilla and beat until smooth. Mix in nuts and apples. Pour in greased and floured tube pan and bake at 350º for 55–60 minutes. Let cool before removing from pan.

Jean Hotz, Corinth Club (Book 1)

Pol's Apple Cake

3 eggs, beaten
1¼ cups oil
2 cups sugar
2½ cups self-rising flour

2 medium apples, peeled and
  chopped
1 cup shredded coconut
1 cup chopped nuts

Blend eggs, oil, and sugar until creamy. Add flour, a little at a time; blend well. Batter will be stiff. Fold in apples, coconut, and nuts. Pour into greased and floured tube pan and bake for 1 hour at 350º. Remove from pan after 30 minutes. Top while cake is warm.

TOPPING:

½ stick butter, softened
½ cup brown sugar

⅓ cup milk

In saucepan, mix butter, sugar, and milk; boil 3 minutes. Pour over warm cake.

Annie Mitchell (Book 3)

Blueberry Cake

2 cups self-rising flour
2 cups sugar
1 teaspoon cinnamon
½ teaspoon ground cloves
3 eggs, beaten
1 cup Wesson oil

2 (6-ounce) jars blueberry
  baby food
1 cup chopped pecans or
  walnuts
1½ cups blueberries

Combine dry ingredients with eggs, oil, and baby food; mix well. Add nuts and blueberries. Pour in greased and floured tube pan or Bundt pan. Bake at 325º for 1 hour.

Bess Lancaster, Grenada, MS (Book 4)

Grace's Apricot Nectar Cake

1 (18¼-ounce) box Duncan
  Hines yellow cake mix
6 eggs, beaten
¾ cup apricot nectar

¾ cup plus 1 tablespoon
  Wesson Oil
1 (3-ounce) package lemon
  Jell-O

Combine cake mix, eggs, apricot nectar, oil, and Jell-O. Pour into greased and floured tube pan. Cook in preheated 350º oven for 45 minutes or until done. Cool slightly and remove from pan.

GLAZE:

2 cups powdered sugar, sifted
¾ cup orange juice

Rind of 1 lemon, grated
Rind of 1 orange, grated

Combine powdered sugar, orange juice, and grated rinds; pour over warm cake. Let cool before serving.

Mildred Lauderdale, Greenwood Council (Book 1)

Peach Custard Cake

¼ cup margarine
½ cup brown sugar
1 (28-ounce) can sliced
   peaches, drained, reserve
   2 teaspoons juice
1 cup chopped nuts (optional)
1 (18¼-ounce) package
   yellow cake mix

½ cup oil
3 eggs
1 (6-ounce) jar peach baby food
½ teaspoon nutmeg
1 (3-ounce) package golden
   egg custard pudding mix

Melt margarine with brown sugar. Add reserved 2 teaspoons peach juice to mixture and pour into greased Bundt pan. Arrange sliced peaches in bottom of pan. Sprinkle with nuts, if desired. Combine remaining ingredients and beat for 3 minutes. Pour on top of peaches and bake at 350º for 45–50 minutes. Cool in pan for 2 minutes; turn out onto serving plate. May be served warm. Can be topped with vanilla ice cream or sweetened whipped cream.

Eloise Freeman, McComb Life Club (Book 1)

Pear Cake

1¼ cups oil
2 cups sugar
3 eggs, separated
1 teaspoon baking soda
2 teaspoons cinnamon
2 teaspoons salt

1 teaspoon baking powder
2½ cups all-purpose flour
3 cups chopped raw pears
1 cup chopped nuts
2 teaspoons vanilla extract

Mix oil, sugar, and egg yolks. Add dry ingredients. Add pears and nuts. Fold in beaten egg whites and vanilla. Bake in greased and floured Bundt pan at 350º for 1 hour.

Anna B. Jackson, Capitol Life Member Club (Book 2)

Crushed Pineapple Cream Cake

1 (18¼-ounce) yellow
  cake mix
4 eggs
1 (5-ounce) box pineapple
  cream instant pudding

¾ cup water
¾ cup Wesson oil
1 (8-ounce) can crushed
  pineapple, drained well,
  reserve juice for Glaze

Mix all ingredients for 2 minutes and pour into greased and floured 9x13-inch pan. Bake 45 minutes at 325º.

GLAZE:

2 tablespoons butter, melted
1 cup confectioners' sugar

Reserved pineapple juice

Mix Glaze ingredients. Remove hot cake from oven when done. Using a fork, prick entire cake and pour on Glaze while warm.

Bessie Fox, Mississippi Telco (Book 2)

Mandarin Orange Cake

Very refreshing!

1 (18¼-ounce) box Duncan
  Hines Butter Recipe Golden
  Cake Mix
¼ cup Crisco Oil

3 eggs
1 (11-ounce) can Mandarin
  oranges, undrained

Mix in order given. Bake in 3 greased and floured layer cake pans at 350° for 20–25 minutes. Let cool before icing.

ICING:

1 (9-ounce) carton frozen Cool
  Whip, thawed
1 (5-ounce) package vanilla
  instant pudding mix

1 (20-ounce) can crushed
  pineapple, drained

Mix in order; whip, and spread on cooled cake. Store in refrigerator.

Ethel Sharp, McComb Life Club (Book 1)

Hummingbird Cake

2 cups all-purpose flour
1 teaspoon salt
1 teaspoon baking soda
1 teaspoon cinnamon
3 eggs
2 cups sugar
1¼ cups oil

1½ teaspoons vanilla extract
1 cup chopped nuts
2 cups chopped bananas
2 cups chopped apples
1 (8-ounce) can crushed
  pineapple
1 cup shredded coconut

Mix dry ingredients in one bowl. Mix eggs, sugar, oil, and vanilla in another bowl; combine mixtures and add nuts, fruit, and coconut. Bake in a greased and floured Bundt pan at 350º for 1 hour and 10 minutes. Cool and remove from pan.

ICING:

1 (8-ounce) package cream
  cheese, softened
1 (4-ounce) stick butter or
  margarine, softened

1 (16-ounce) box confectioners'
  sugar
1 teaspoon vanilla extract

Beat all ingredients until creamy. Spread on cooled cake.

Mrs. Inez Halford, Greenville Club (Book 1)

The first rotary dial telephone was developed in 1923 by Antoine Barnay in France.

Strawberry Pecan Cake

1 (18¼-ounce) box white cake
   mix
4 eggs
½ cup milk
1 (3-ounce) package strawberry
   Jell-O
1 cup flaked coconut
½ cup Wesson oil
1 cup frozen strawberries,
   thawed
1 cup chopped pecans

Mix together all ingredients and bake in 3 or 4 greased and floured cake pans at 350° for 20–25 minutes or until done.

FROSTING:

1 (16-ounce) box confectioners'
   sugar
1 stick margarine, softened
½ cup drained strawberries
½ cup shredded coconut
½ cup chopped pecans

Cream sugar and margarine, add other ingredients; ice cake.

Note: If Frosting is too stiff, add small amount of sweet milk or juice from strawberries.

Frances H. Welch, Mendenhall, MS (Book 4)

Jam Cake

1 cup butter, softened
2 cups sugar
6 eggs, separated
2 cups seedless blackberry jam
4 cups all-purpose flour, sifted
1 teaspoon cinnamon
1 teaspoon nutmeg
2 teaspoons baking soda
½ cup sour cream

Cream butter and sugar until light and fluffy; beat egg yolks in one at a time; mix well. Stir in jam; add flour sifted twice with spices and baking soda, alternately with sour cream, ending with flour. Fold in beaten egg whites. Bake in 3 or 4 greased and floured 9-inch cake pans in 350° oven until done, about 20 minutes. Cool. Fill and ice with your favorite cream icing or divinity icing.

Betty Davidson Upton by Patsy Tolleson, Jackson, MS (Book 4)

Three-Day Easy Coconut Cake

1 (18¼-ounce) box white cake
  mix
2 (4½-ounce) packages
  frozen coconut

2 (8-ounce) cartons sour cream
2 cups sugar
1 (8-ounce) carton frozen
  whipped topping, thawed

Prepare cake according to package directions. Bake in 2 greased and floured layer cake pans at 350° for 30–35 minutes; cool, then split into 4 layers. Mix frozen coconut with sour cream and sugar. Set aside ½ cup of this mixture for later use; spread the rest between layers. Mix reserved ½ cup coconut mixture with whipped topping; spread on top and sides. Refrigerate 3 days in an airtight container before cutting.

Mary Cooper, Jackson South Council (Book 1)

Coco Lopez Coconut Cake

1 (18¼-ounce) package
  Duncan Hines Deluxe II
  yellow cake mix
1 (14-ounce) can sweetened
  condensed milk
1 (15-ounce) can Coco Lopez
  cream of coconut

1 (8-ounce) container frozen Cool
  Whip, thawed
1 (6-ounce) package frozen
  coconut

Prepare cake and bake in 9x13-inch pan according to package directions. Cool 20–30 minutes. Leave cake in pan and poke holes through top of cake with fork; space holes about 1 inch apart. Slowly pour Coco Lopez over cake, then condensed milk. Cover with foil and refrigerate overnight.

Next day, spread Cool Whip over cake and sprinkle coconut over top of Cool Whip.

Gail Rushing, Natchez Council (Book 2)

Bell's Light Fruit Cake

1½ cups butter, softened
  (sweet is best)
1½ cups sugar
1 tablespoon vanilla extract
¼ cup brandy (optional)
1 teaspoon lemon juice
7 eggs, separated, room
  temperature
3½ cups all-purpose flour,
  divided

3 cups chopped candied yellow
  and green pineapple
2 cups chopped candied red
  and green cherries
½ cup chopped candied citron
1½ cups golden raisins
3 cups pecan halves

Cream butter and sugar until light and fluffy; stir in vanilla, brandy, if desired, and lemon juice. Beat egg yolks. Add beaten egg yolks and 3 cups flour to creamed mixture. Combine candied fruit, raisins, and nuts in large mixing bowl. Dredge with remaining ½ cup flour, stirring to coat well. Stir mixture into batter. Beat egg whites until stiff, then fold into batter. Line bottom of 3 greased and floured 9x5x3-inch loaf pans with wax paper; spoon batter into pans. Arrange additional fruit and nuts on top as desired. Bake at 250º for 1½ hours or until done.

Option: You may bake at 250º in a greased and floured Bundt pan for 2½–3 hours.

Fay Lambert, Greenwood Council (Book 1)

Mama's White Fruit Cake

2 sticks butter, softened
1½ cups sugar
6 eggs
3 cups all-purpose flour
⅛ teaspoon baking soda
1½ cups pitted dates, chopped

2 cups candied pineapple,
    chopped
4 cups pecans, chopped
½ teaspoon vanilla extract
½ teaspoon almond extract

Cream butter and sugar; add eggs, one at a time. Add other ingredients in order. Bake in slow oven (about 250º) for 1½–2 hours or until straw comes out clean. Cool and wrap; good for 3–4 weeks.

E. W. Roney, Laurel, MS (Book 4)

Fruit Cocktail Cake

½ stick margarine
1½ cups white sugar
2 eggs
2 cups all-purpose flour

1½ teaspoons baking soda
1 (15-ounce) can fruit cocktail,
    undrained
½ cup brown sugar

Cream margarine and white sugar; add eggs and beat well. Sift flour and baking soda; add to mixture. Stir in fruit cocktail. Pour into greased and floured 9x13-inch baking pan. Sprinkle with brown sugar. Bake at 350º for 25–30 minutes. Spread with hot Icing while still warm.

ICING:
½ cup evaporated milk
¾ cup sugar
1 teaspoon vanilla extract

1 stick margarine
1 cup chopped pecans
1 (3½-ounce) can flaked coconut

Mix milk, sugar, vanilla, and margarine; boil 2 minutes, stirring constantly. Add pecans and coconut. Cover cake while Icing is still hot.

Gail Lang, Meridian Council (Book 1)

Dump Cake

1 (20-ounce) can crushed
    pineapple, undrained
1 (32-ounce) can cherry pie
    filling
1 (18¼-ounce) box yellow cake
    mix

2 sticks margarine,
    thinly sliced
½ cup chopped nuts

Spread crushed pineapple into bottom of a greased 9x13-inch buttered baking pan. Layer cherry pie filling on pineapple, then cake mix on filling, then margarine to cover the entire top. Top with chopped nuts. Bake at 350º for 55 minutes.

Mrs. Bill Robinson, Gulf Coast Council (Book 1)

Boiler Cake

1 stick margarine
½ cup Crisco shortening
1 cup water
3 tablespoons cocoa
2 cups all-purpose flour

2 cups sugar
½ cup buttermilk
1 teaspoon baking soda
2 eggs, beaten
1 teaspoon vanilla extract

In boiler, put margarine, Crisco, water, and cocoa. Bring to a boil, then add flour and sugar. Add buttermilk mixed with baking soda. Add eggs and vanilla. Pour into greased 9x13-inch pan and bake 25 minutes at 400º.

ICING:

1 stick margarine
5 tablespoons milk
3 tablespoons cocoa

1 (16-ounce) box confectioners'
    sugar

Bring margarine, milk, and cocoa to a boil, then mix in confectioners' sugar. Spread on cake.

Mrs. Don Moulder, Jackson South Council (Book 2)

Can't Miss White Cake

2 cups sugar
¾ cup butter, softened
2½ cups all-purpose flour,
1 teaspoon salt

2½ teaspoons baking powder
1 cup milk
1 teaspoon vanilla extract
5 egg whites, beaten

Cream sugar and butter well. Sift flour, salt, and baking powder together; mix very well. Add flour mixture to sugar and butter mixture; add milk, vanilla, and beaten egg whites. Bake in 2 greased and floured cake pans at 350º for 25–30 minutes or until done. Frost with your favorite icing.

Mildred Lauderdale, Greenwood Council (Book 1)

Gooey Butter Cake

1 (18¼-ounce) box yellow cake
  mix
3 eggs, divided
½ cup butter or margarine,
  softened

½ cup chopped pecans
1 (8-ounce) package cream
  cheese, softened
1 (16-ounce) box powdered sugar
1 (7-ounce) can flaked coconut

Combine dry cake mix, 1 egg, and butter, then add pecans. Press into a greased 9x13-inch pan. Mix together remaining 2 eggs, cream cheese, powdered sugar, and coconut. Pour over cake mixture in pan. Bake for 40–45 minutes at 350º. Cut into small squares.

Barbara Evans, Meridian Council (Book 1)

Italian Cream Cake

1 stick margarine
½ cup vegetable shortening
2 cups sugar
5 eggs, separated
2 cups all-purpose flour
1 teaspoon baking soda

1 cup buttermilk
1 teaspoon vanilla extract
1 (4½-ounce) package frozen
  coconut
1 cup chopped pecans

Cream margarine and shortening; add sugar and beat until mixture is smooth. Add egg yolks and beat well. Combine flour and baking soda; add to creamed mixture alternately with buttermilk. Stir in vanilla extract. Add coconut and nuts. Fold in stiffly beaten egg whites. Pour batter into 3 greased and floured 8-inch cake pans. Bake at 350º for 25 minutes.

FROSTING:

1 (8-ounce) package cream
  cheese, softened
1 stick margarine, softened
1 (16-ounce) box confectioners'
  sugar

1 teaspoon vanilla extract
1 cup chopped pecans

Beat cream cheese and margarine until smooth. Add confectioners' sugar; mix well. Add vanilla and beat until smooth. Stir in pecans. Spread on cool cake.

Tena Rayborn, Hattiesburg Council (Book 1)

Rum Cake

1 cup chopped pecans	1 cup vegetable oil
1 (18¼-ounce) box yellow cake mix	4 eggs, beaten
	½ cup cold water
1 (5-ounce) package vanilla instant pudding	½ cup dark rum

Preheat oven to 325º. Grease and flour a 9- or 10-inch tube pan. Sprinkle pecans over bottom of pan. Combine cake mix, pudding mix, oil, eggs, water, and rum. Pour batter over pecans. Bake for 1 hour. Let cool and invert onto plate. Prick top (use toothpicks or an ice pick). Drizzle and brush Glaze over top.

GLAZE:

1 stick butter	1 cup granulated sugar
¼ cup water	½ cup dark rum

Melt butter; stir in water and sugar. Boil 5 minutes, stirring constantly; stir in rum. Glaze cake.

Nervetta Fairchild, Hattiesburg Life Member Club; Arnell W. Patterson, Clarksdale Club; Mary F. Reach, Jackson South Council
(Book 1)

The mobile telephone was invented by Bell Telephone Company and introduced into New York City police cars in 1924. Although the first commercial mobile telephone service became available in St. Louis, Missouri, in 1946, the mobile telephone would not become common for another four decades.

Red Velvet Cake

1 cup vegetable shortening	1 tablespoon cocoa
1¼ cups sugar	1 cup buttermilk
2 eggs, well beaten	1 (2-ounce) bottle red food
1 teaspoon vanilla extract	coloring
2¼ cups all-purpose flour	1 teaspoon baking soda
1 teaspoon salt	1 tablespoon vinegar

Cream shortening and sugar; add beaten eggs and vanilla. Sift flour, salt, and cocoa 3 times. Add to egg mixture, alternately with buttermilk. Blend in food coloring. Dissolve baking soda in vinegar. Fold into batter. Pour into 3 wax paper-lined layer cake pans; bake in 350° oven for 20–25 minutes.

FROSTING:

1 cup milk	1 stick butter, softened
¼ cup flour	1 cup sugar
Dash of salt	1 teaspoon vanilla
½ cup shortening	Coconut for topping (optional)

Cook milk, flour, and salt over low flame to pudding stage, stirring constantly. Cool in refrigerator. Cream shortening, margarine, and sugar until fluffy; add vanilla. Blend in cooled pudding mixture. Beat well until it looks like whipped cream. Spread on cake; sprinkle with coconut, if desired.

Mildred Thompson, Meridian Council; Ouva Green, Meridian Life Member Club; Mrs. Curtiss (Hattie) Hale, Columbus Club (Book 1)

Coca-Cola Cake

2 cups all-purpose flour
2 cups sugar
2 sticks margarine
3 tablespoons cocoa
1 cup Coca-Cola

½ teaspoon baking soda
½ cup buttermilk
2 eggs, beaten
1 teaspoon vanilla extract
½ cup miniature marshmallows

Mix flour and sugar. In a pan, mix margarine, cocoa, and cola. Bring to a boil, then pour over sugar-flour mixture; mix. Add baking soda to buttermilk and allow to foam. Set this aside. Add eggs, vanilla, and marshmallows to sugar-flour mixture. Add the buttermilk and soda. Bake 30–40 minutes at 350º in greased 9x13-inch pan.

ICING:

1 stick margarine
3 tablespoons cocoa
6 tablespoons Coca-Cola

1 (16-ounce) box powdered
   sugar
1 cup chopped pecans

Bring first 3 ingredients to a boil; pour over powdered sugar . Beat and add pecans. Spread over cake while warm.

Gail Self, Future Pioneer, Greenwood Council (Book 2)

Chocolate Cookie Sheet Cake

2½ cups all-purpose flour
2 cups sugar
½ teaspoon salt
2 sticks margarine
1 cup water

3 tablespoons cocoa
2 eggs, well beaten
1 teaspoon baking soda
½ cup buttermilk
1 teaspoon vanilla extract

Sift flour; mix with sugar and salt. In saucepan, put margarine, water, and cocoa. Bring to a boil and pour over flour mixture. In a separate bowl, combine eggs, baking soda, buttermilk, and vanilla. Add to cocoa mixture; mix well. Bake at 350º for 20 minutes in greased sheet cake pan.

ICING:

1 stick butter
3 tablespoons cocoa
6 tablespoons milk
1 (16-ounce) box confectioners'
  sugar

½ cup chopped pecans
1 teaspoon vanilla extract

Mix butter, cocoa, and milk in saucepan. Heat on low flame; do not boil. Remove from heat; add sugar, pecans, and vanilla. Frost cake as soon as removed from oven.

Ethel Comeaux, Gulf Coast Council (Book 1)

Old-Fashioned Chocolate Cake

½ cup cocoa powder
½ cup boiling water
⅔ cup shortening
1¾ cups sugar
1 teaspoon vanilla extract

2 eggs
2¼ cups all-purpose flour
1½ teaspoons baking soda
½ teaspoon salt (optional)
1⅓ cups buttermilk

Preheat oven to 350º. In small bowl, stir together cocoa and boiling water until smooth; set aside. In larger mixer bowl, cream shortening, sugar, and vanilla until light and fluffy. Add eggs; beat well. Combine flour, baking soda, and salt, if desired; add alternately with buttermilk to creamed mixture. Blend in cocoa mixture. Pour into 2 greased and floured 9-inch cake pans. Bake 35–40 minutes or until wooden pick inserted into center comes out clean. Cool 10 minutes; remove from pans. Cool completely; frost with Chocolate Butter Cream Frosting.

CHOCOLATE BUTTER CREAM FROSTING:
6 tablespoons butter or
  margarine, softened
2⅔ cups powdered sugar

½ cup cocoa powder
⅓ cup milk
1 teaspoon vanilla extract

In small mixer bowl, cream butter. Add powdered sugar, cocoa powder, and milk; beat to spreading consistency (additional milk may be needed). Blend in vanilla extract, and ice cooled cake.

Sarah C. Bennett, Jackson, MS (Book 4)

German Chocolate Cake

1 package German's sweet chocolate	1 teaspoon vanilla
½ cup boiling water	½ teaspoon salt
1 cup butter	1 teaspoon baking soda
2 cups sugar	2½ cups sifted cake flour
4 eggs, separated	1 cup buttermilk

Melt chocolate in ½ cup boiling water; cool. Cream butter and sugar until light and fluffy. Add egg yolks, 1 at a time, and beat well after each. Add melted chocolate mixture and vanilla. Mix well. Sift together salt, soda, and flour, then add alternately with buttermilk to chocolate mixture, beating well. Beat until smooth. Beat egg whites until stiff peaks form. Fold into batter. Pour into 3 (8- or 9-inch) cake pans, lined on bottom with wax paper. Bake in 350° oven for 35–40 minutes. Cool. Frost tops only with Coconut-Pecan Frosting.

COCONUT-PECAN FROSTING:

1 cup evaporated milk	1 teaspoon vanilla
1 cup sugar	1⅓ cups flaked coconut
3 egg yolks	1 cup chopped pecans
½ pound margarine	

Combine milk, sugar, egg yolks, and margarine in saucepan; add vanilla. Cook and stir over medium heat until mixture thickens (takes about 12 minutes). Add coconut and pecans. Beat until frosting is cool and thick enough to spread.

Kent Holden, Jackson North Council (Book 1)

Cheese Cake

2 (8-ounce) packages cream
cheese, room temperature
¾ cup sugar
2 eggs, room temperature
1½ teaspoons vanilla

1 graham cracker pie crust
1 (8-ounce) carton sour cream
1½ teaspoons vanilla extract
¼ cup sugar

Combine first 4 ingredients and beat until smooth. Pour into crust and bake at 350º for 18 minutes. Combine sour cream, vanilla, and sugar by gently folding; spoon over cheesecake. Return to oven for 5 minutes. Use topping of your choice, or Praline Topping.

PRALINE TOPPING:

1 cup dark corn syrup
¼ cup cornstarch

2 cups brown sugar
1 teaspoon vanilla extract

Combine corn syrup, cornstarch, and brown sugar in a small saucepan. Cook and stir until thickened and bubbly. Remove from heat; stir in vanilla. Cool slightly. To serve, spoon some of the warm Topping over the cheese cake. Pass remaining sauce to guests for a little extra topping! Makes 12–16 servings.

C. Q. and Birdie Hamilton, Natchez Council (Book 1)

Triple-Layered
Lemon Cheesecake

A luscious cake with an almost fluffy texture. The sweetness is toned down perfectly by the tartness of the lemon.

CRUST:

2 cups cinnamon graham
  cracker crumbs
2 cups chopped walnuts

6 tablespoons butter, melted
2 tablespoons sugar

Preheat oven to 350°. Combine ingredients thoroughly. Press Crust evenly onto the bottom and sides of buttered 9-inch spring-form pan. Bake for 5 minutes. Cool.

FILLING:

3 (8-ounce) packages cream
  cheese, softened
¾ cup sugar
3 eggs

¼ cup lemon juice
2 teaspoons grated lemon rind
1 teaspoon vanilla extract

Beat cream cheese until soft. Add sugar, blending thoroughly. Add eggs, one at a time, beating well after each addition. Mix in lemon juice, grated rind, and vanilla. Blend well. Pour over Crust. Bake for 35 minutes.

TOPPING:

2 cups sour cream
3 tablespoons sugar

2 teaspoons vanilla extract

While cake is baking, blend sour cream, sugar, and vanilla. Remove cake from oven. Gently spread on Topping. Return to oven and bake for 12 minutes; cool on rack for 30 minutes. Makes 16–20 servings.

Sheila Moore (Book 3)

Chocolate Chip Cheesecake

1½ cups (about 18) finely
 crushed cream-filled
 chocolate sandwich cookies
2–3 tablespoons butter or
 margarine, melted
3 (8-ounce) packages cream
 cheese, softened
1 (14-ounce) can sweetened
 condensed milk
3 eggs
2 teaspoons vanilla extract
1 cup mini chocolate chips,
 divided
1 tablespoon flour

Combine cookie crumbs and butter; press firmly on bottom of greased 9-inch springform pan. Beat cream cheese until fluffy; gradually beat in condensed milk until smooth. Add eggs and vanilla; mix well. Toss ½ cup chips with flour to coat; stir into cheese mixture. Pour into pan; sprinkle remaining ½ cup chips evenly over top. Bake in a 350º preheated oven for 1 hour. Cool; chill thoroughly. Serves 8.

Nella Duckworth (Book 3)

Caramel Icing

This is a simple, easy caramel icing. No more burnt sugar to make caramel.

½ cup buttermilk
2 cups sugar
¾ cup margarine
½ teaspoon baking soda
1 tablespoon light Karo syrup
12 large marshmallows, or
 1 cup small marshmallows

Mix all ingredients together in boiler over low to medium heat; cook to firm-ball stage (248º); beat well and pour on cake of your choice.

Lou Sparks, Jackson South Council (Book 1)

Cream Cheese Frosting

1 (8-ounce) package cream
  cheese, softened
1 stick butter or margarine,
  softened

2 (16-ounce) packages
  confectioners' sugar
2 teaspoons vanilla extract

Combine cream cheese and butter; cream until smooth. Add confectioners' sugar, beating until light and fluffy. Stir in vanilla. Makes enough for a 3-layer cake.

Travis E. Johnson, Hattiesburg Council (Book 1)

Peanut Butter Frosting

2½ cups sugar
1 cup milk
2 tablespoons margarine

1 cup peanut butter
  (smooth or crunchy)

Bring sugar, milk, and margarine to a boil, stirring constantly, until it forms a soft ball in cold water. Remove from heat; add peanut butter. Beat with a spoon. Spread on a 2-layer cake. Enjoy!

Virginia B. Frasier, Sallis, MS (Book 4)

Never Fail Seven Minute Frosting

3 egg whites
1½ cups Karo syrup

¼ teaspoon cream of tartar
9 large marshmallows

Cook first 3 ingredients in double boiler, beating constantly until peaks form. Add marshmallows and beat until of spreading consistency.

Teresa Wade, Jackson South Council (Book 2)

Cookies and Candies

1968
Trimline

The twelve-button Touch-Tone Trimline was dramatically different from any other phone at the time. With the first ever dial-in-handset, it allowed people to dial a new call without returning to the base of the phone. The design of the phone later paved the way for today's cordless and cellular phones. Although only ten buttons were needed for ordinary dialing, the two "extra" buttons (the * and # keys) were added for advanced services and for dialing international phone calls. The first Touch-Tone Trimline phone had round buttons instead of square. The convenience of having the dial in the handset was especially handy in the wall-mount model. The Trimline model also introduced the concept of modular plugs. Also in 1968, 911 was introduced as a nationwide emergency number.

Fruit Delight Cookies

4 cups dates, chopped
1⅓ cups candied cherries, chopped
1⅓ cups candied pineapple, chopped
4 cups nuts, chopped
2½ cups all-purpose flour, sifted and measured
1 teaspoon baking soda
1 teaspoon salt
1 teaspoon cinnamon
1 cup butter or margarine, softened
1½ cups sugar
2 eggs

Combine fruits and nuts; set aside. Combine flour, baking soda, salt, and cinnamon; set aside. Cream butter and sugar; add eggs and beat well. Mix part of the flour mixture with fruit and add remaining flour mixture to creamed mixture. Stir in fruit; mix well. Drop by teaspoonfuls onto greased cookie sheet. Bake at 350º for 10–15 minutes.

Francis Kirkpatrick, Tupelo Council (Book 1)

Pineapple Cookies

1 cup shortening
1½ cups sugar
1 egg
3½ cups all-purpose flour
1 teaspoon baking soda
½ teaspoon salt
¼ teaspoon nutmeg
1 (8-ounce) can crushed pineapple, with juice
½ cup chopped nuts

Mix shortening, sugar, and egg. Sift dry ingredients together and stir into shortening mixture. Add pineapple and nuts. Drop by teaspoonfuls about 2 inches apart on lightly greased baking sheet. Bake at 400º for 8–10 minutes. Makes about 5 dozen cookies.

Dot Trinkner, Jackson North Council (Book 1)

Date Pinwheel Cookies

DOUGH:

½ cup butter, softened
½ cup brown sugar
½ cup granulated sugar
½ teaspoon vanilla extract

1 egg
2 cups sifted all-purpose flour
¼ teaspoon baking soda
¼ teaspoon salt

Cream butter, brown sugar, granulated sugar, vanilla, and egg. Beat until light and fluffy. Add dry ingredients and mix well. Chill until firm enough to roll (about 30 minutes).

FILLING:

1 (7.25-ounce) package pitted
   dates, chopped
¼ cup granulated sugar

Dash of salt
⅓ cup water
1 cup chopped pecans

Bring dates to a boil with sugar, salt, and water. Simmer for 5 minutes; stirring often. Add nuts and allow to cool.

Halve the Dough and roll each portion on wax paper into a 9x12-inch rectangle. Spread with Filling. Roll up tightly from the end. Wrap in wax paper and chill overnight. Slice ⅛ inch thick and bake in 370º oven for 10 minutes.

Nellie Williams, Gulf Coast Council (Book 2)

Zucchini Cookies

1 cup sugar
1 stick butter or margarine,
  softened
1 egg
2 cups all-purpose flour
1 teaspoon baking soda
1 teaspoon cinnamon

½ teaspoon ground cloves
½ teaspoon salt
1 cup grated zucchini
  (do not peel)
1 teaspoon vanilla extract
½ cup chopped nuts
1 cup golden raisins

Mix sugar, butter, and egg until fluffy. Add dry ingredients and mix well. Add zucchini, vanilla, nuts, and raisins. Drop by teaspoonfuls onto a greased cookie sheet. Bake at 350º for 12–14 minutes or until brown. Do not drop too close together.

Note: You can also make a loaf of bread with this recipe.

Fredonia Granholm, Grenada, MS (Book 4)

Emma's Gingersnaps

¾ cup oil
1¼ cups sugar, divided
1 egg
4 tablespoons molasses
2 cups all-purpose flour

½ teaspoon salt
1 teaspoon cinnamon
2 teaspoons baking soda
1 teaspoon ginger

Mix oil and 1 cup sugar; add egg and mix. Stir in molasses. Sift dry ingredients, except remaining ¼ cup sugar, and add. Beat well. Drop by teaspoon into reserved sugar; make balls and place on lightly greased cookie sheet. Slightly flatten with fork. Bake for 15 minutes at 350º.

Kathy LaMonte, Jackson, MS (Book 3)

Molasses Cookies

½ cup shortening
1 cup sugar
2 eggs
1¼ cups molasses
4 cups all-purpose flour

2 teaspoons baking soda
½ teaspoon salt
1 teaspoon ginger
1 teaspoon cinnamon
½ cup buttermilk

Cream shortening and sugar; add eggs and molasses, and mix well. Combine dry ingredients. Add to creamed mixture alternately with buttermilk, beginning and ending with flour mixture. Drop dough by teaspoonfuls, 1½ inches apart, onto lightly greased cookie sheet. Bake at 350º for 10–12 minutes.

Frances Barnes, Life Member Club, Tupelo, MS (Book 4)

Chocolate Cookies

½ cup oil
3 (1-ounce) squares
  unsweetened chocolate,
  melted
2 cups sugar
4 eggs

2 teaspoons vanilla extract
½ teaspoon salt
2 cups all-purpose flour
2 teaspoons baking powder
Confectioners' sugar

Mix oil, melted chocolate, and sugar. Beat in eggs 1 at a time; add vanilla. Stir in salt, flour, and baking powder. Mix well. Chill several hours or overnight. When ready to bake, roll by teaspoonfuls into balls in confectioners' sugar. Put on ungreased cookie sheet and bake 10–12 minutes at 350º.

Mary Alice Hydrick, Jackson North Council (Book 2)

Hershey's Great American Chocolate Chip Cookies

1 cup butter, softened
¾ cup sugar
¾ cup light brown sugar, packed
1 teaspoon vanilla extract
2 eggs
2¼ cups all-purpose flour, unsifted

1 teaspoon baking soda
½ teaspoon salt
2 cups (12 ounces) Hershey's semisweet chocolate chip
1 cup chopped nuts

Cream together butter, sugar, brown sugar, and vanilla until light and fluffy. Add eggs and beat well. Combine flour, baking soda, and salt; gradually beat into creamed mixture. Stir in chocolate chips and nuts. Drop by teaspoonfuls onto ungreased cookie sheet. Bake at 375º for 8–10 minutes or until lightly brown. Cool and serve. Makes 6 dozen 2½-inch cookies.

Sue Hatton (Book 3)

Party Cookies

1 cup shortening
1 cup brown sugar
½ cup granulated sugar
2 teaspoons vanilla extract

2 eggs
2¼ cups sifted all-purpose flour
½ cup M&Ms

Blend shortening and sugars. Beat in vanilla and eggs. Sift flour and add to the sugar-egg mixture; mix well. Stir in most of M&M candies, reserving some candies for decorating. Drop from teaspoon onto ungreased cookie sheet. Decorate tops of cookies with remaining M&Ms. Bake at 375º for 10–12 minutes, until golden brown.

Catherine Waldrop, Tupelo Council (Book 2)

Peanut Butter Cookies

1 cup shortening
1 cup granulated sugar
1 cup brown sugar
2 eggs, beaten
1 teaspoon vanilla extract

1 cup peanut butter (crunchy
  is best)
2½ cups all-purpose flour
2 teaspoons baking soda
Dash of salt

Cream shortening and sugars; add eggs and vanilla; stir in peanut butter. Sift in remaining dry ingredients and mix thoroughly. Roll into 2-inch balls and place on greased cookie sheets. Press with fork in crisscross designs. Bake at 375º for about 10 minutes.

Azelie Jones, Tupelo Council (Book 2)

Oatmeal Peanut Butter Cookies

2 cups quick oats
1 cup all-purpose flour, sifted
1 teaspoon baking powder
1 teaspoon baking soda
1 teaspoon salt
1 cup peanut butter

¾ cup margarine, softened
1 cup firmly packed brown
  sugar
½ cup sugar
2 eggs
2 teaspoons vanilla extract

Stir together oats, flour, baking powder, baking soda, and salt. In large bowl, beat peanut butter and margarine until smooth. Beat in sugars. Beat eggs and vanilla into peanut butter mixture. Add oat mixture to peanut butter mixture. If necessary, chill dough. Shape into 1-inch balls. Place on greased cookie sheet 2 inches apart. Flatten with floured fork, making crisscross pattern. Bake in 350º oven for 8–10 minutes. Cool on wire rack. Makes 6 dozen cookies.

Robbie Walters (Book 2)

Oatmeal Cookies

2 sticks margarine, softened
1 cup brown sugar
1 cup granulated sugar
2 eggs, well beaten
1½ cups plain flour, sifted

1 teaspoon salt
1 teaspoon baking soda
2 teaspoons vanilla extract
3 cups oatmeal
1 cup chopped pecans

Preheat oven to 350º. Cream margarine and sugars; gradually add eggs. Mix together flour, salt, and baking soda; mix well. Add vanilla, then oatmeal and pecans. Drop by spoonfuls onto cookie sheet and bake about 10 minutes until light brown.

Eva Suggs (Book 3)

One-Cup Cookies

1 cup butter, softened
1 cup brown sugar
1 cup white sugar
1 cup oil
1 egg
1 teaspoon vanilla flavoring

4 cups self-rising flour
1 cup oatmeal, uncooked
1 cup Rice Krispies
1 cup flaked coconut
1 cup chopped pecans

Mix butter, sugars, oil, and egg. Add vanilla. Add remaining ingredients; mix well. Drop by spoonfuls onto cookie sheet and bake in a 350º oven for 10 minutes.

Brenda V. Snowden (Book 3)

Sugar Cookies

1 cup margarine
1 cup granulated sugar
1 cup Wesson oil
2 eggs
4 cups plus 4 tablespoons
  all-purpose flour

1 teaspoon baking soda
1 teaspoon cream of tartar
1 teaspoon vanilla flavoring
1 teaspoon lemon flavoring

Cream together margarine, sugar, and oil. Add eggs and beat well. Sift together flour, baking soda, and cream of tartar; add to creamed mixture. Add flavorings and mix well; chill.

Make into small balls and place on greased cookie sheet. Rub bottom of drinking glass with oil and dip in granulated sugar. Press each ball flat. Bake for 10 minutes at 375º. Remove from cookie sheet immediately.

Margaret Nail, Tupelo Council (Book 3)

White Cookies

1 stick butter, softened
2 tablespoons sugar
1 cup cake flour

1 cup ground pecans
1 teaspoon vanilla flavoring
Confectioners' sugar

Beat butter and sugar until creamy. Add cake flour, ground pecans, and vanilla; mix well. Roll dough into balls, using approximately 1 tablespoon mixture for each ball. Bake on cookie sheet at 300º for 4–5 minutes, or until done. Roll in sifted confectioners' sugar while hot. Roll again when cold.

Note: Texture will differ with chopped pecans—better results with ground pecans.

Margie Sasser, Edwards, MS (Book 3)

Never Fail Drop Cookies

1 cup granulated sugar*　　1 teaspoon vanilla extract
1 egg　　½ cup butter or oil
2 tablespoons milk　　1½ cups flour

Mix first 5 ingredients. Add flour. Mix well. Drop by tablespoonfuls onto cookie sheet. Bake at 375º for 10–12 minutes. Coconut or
nuts may be added, if desired.

*Can substitute ¾ cup brown sugar and ½ cup granulated sugar.

Mrs. W. G. Morgan, Greenwood Council (Book 1)

Swedish Heirloom Cookies

2 sticks butter or margarine,　　1 tablespoon water
　softened　　⅛ teaspoon salt
1 cup powdered sugar　　1 cup chopped nuts
2 cups all-purpose flour　　Additional powdered sugar
1 tablespoon vanilla extract

Cream butter and powdered sugar together; add flour, vanilla,
water, salt, and nuts. Roll in little balls and press down with fingers. Bake on greased cookie sheet in 350º oven until slightly
brown, 12–15 minutes. While hot, roll cookies in powdered sugar.

Mattie McMinn, Gulf Coast Council (Book 1)

Tea Cakes

Tastes like Mama's.

½ cup butter or margarine, softened
1 cup sugar
1 egg
2 tablespoons ice water
1 teaspoon vanilla extract

1¼ cups all-purpose flour
1 teaspoon cream of tartar (must have!)
½ teaspoon baking soda
¼ teaspoon salt

Cream butter and sugar until fluffy. Add egg, water, and vanilla. Mix dry ingredients together and gradually mix in with wet ingredients. Chill 40 minutes (important). Roll very thin on floured board and cut out. Bake at 350º for about 8 minutes, until brown.

Earine Robertson, Jackson North Council (Book 2)

Tea Cakes

2 cups sugar
1 cup Crisco or margarine
3 eggs
1½ teaspoons baking powder

1 teaspoon vanilla extract
1 tablespoon milk
4 cups self-rising flour

Cream sugar and shortening together; add eggs, one at a time. Add baking powder, vanilla, milk, and flour; mix well. Roll into small balls and place on greased cookie sheets; flatten with fingers. Bake at 325º for 10–12 minutes or until light brown around the edges. Makes 4½ dozen cookies.

Elizabeth Butler (Book 3)

Cream Cheese Cookies

¼ cup butter or margarine,
  softened
1 (8-ounce) package cream
  cheese, softened

1 egg yolk
¼ teaspoon vanilla extract
1 (18¼-ounce) box yellow
  or devil's food cake mix

Cream butter and cream cheese together. Blend in egg yolk and vanilla. Add dry cake mix (⅓ at a time), mixing well after each addition. (If mixer is used, add last third of cake mix and mix by hand). Cover; chill for 30 minutes.

Heat oven to 375º. Drop by level teaspoonfuls onto greased baking sheet. Bake 8–10 minutes or until golden brown. Cool slightly before removing from sheet. Yields 6–8 dozen cookies.

Mary Narup Shank, Jackson, MS (Book 4)

Chess Squares

1 stick margarine, softened
1 (18¼-ounce) box yellow
  cake mix
4 eggs, divided
1 (8-ounce) package cream
  cheese, softened

1 (16-ounce) package
  confectioners' sugar
1 teaspoon vanilla extract

Mix together until crumbly, the margarine, cake mix, and 1 egg. Press into greased 9x13x2-inch pan. Cream until fluffy, the cream cheese, confectioners' sugar, vanilla, and remaining 3 eggs. Pour over crumb crust. Bake at 325º for 45 minutes until golden brown. Cool and cut into squares.

Bernice Passons and Cindy Davidson, Jackson South Council
(Book 1)

Heavenly Hash

Number of calories? Don't count them!

1 egg	1 stick butter, melted
1 cup sugar	½ teaspoon baking powder
¾ cup plain cake flour	1 cup broken pecans
2 tablespoons cocoa	Miniature marshmallows

Mix all ingredients, except pecans and marshmallows. Put in greased 8x8x2-inch cake pan. Top with pecans. Bake at 320º for about 30 minutes. While still hot, top with marshmallows; cover and put in oven till marshmallows melt.

ICING:

½ cup evaporated milk	1 (16-ounce) box confectioners'
¼ stick butter, melted	sugar
2 tablespoons cocoa	

Beat together milk and melted butter. Add cocoa and confectioners' sugar. Beat until as thick as desired and pour over melted marshmallows. There will be plenty of icing.

Janet L. Steffen (Book 3)

Lemon Squares

1 cup all-purpose flour	2 eggs, beaten
½ cup confectioners' sugar	1 cup sugar
½ cup butter or margarine	Dash of salt
2 tablespoons lemon juice	½ teaspoon baking powder
1 lemon rind, ground fine	2 tablespoons all-purpose flour

Blend the flour, confectioners' sugar, and butter; spread on greased 9x13-inch baking pan up to the edges. Bake at 350º for 25 minutes.

Combine lemon juice, lemon rind, eggs, sugar, salt, baking powder, and flour; pour over pastry. Bake at 350º for 25 minutes. Cool.

GLAZE:

Juice of 1 lemon	Powdered sugar

Make glaze with the lemon juice and powdered sugar to make the consistency of mayonnaise. Pour over cooled lemon squares and serve.

Annie L. Beard, Jackson Council North (Book 1)

 The first Picturephone test system, built in 1956, was crude—it transmitted an image only once every two seconds. By 1964 a complete experimental system, the "Mod 1," had been developed, but failed miserably. It wasn't until decades later, with improvements in speed, resolution, miniaturization, and the incorporation of Picturephone into another piece of desktop equipment, the computer, that the promise of a personal video communication system was realized.

Sunburst Lemon Bars

CRUST:

2 cups all-purpose flour
½ cup confectioners' sugar
1 cup butter, softened

1 teaspoon baking powder
¼ cup lemon juice

In large bowl, combine Crust ingredients. Beat at low speed until crumbly. Press mixture evenly in bottom of ungreased 9x13-inch pan. Bake at 350º for 20–30 minutes.

FILLING:

4 eggs
2 cups sugar

¼ cup flour

In large bowl, combine Filling ingredients; mix well. Pour mixture over warm Crust. Return to oven and bake for 25–30 minutes. Cool completely.

GLAZE:

1 cup confectioners' sugar

3 tablespoons lemon juice

In small bowl, combine Glaze ingredients; blend until smooth. Drizzle over cooled bars. Cut into bars. Makes 36.

Martha Overton, Natchez (Book 3)

Butterscotch Brownie Pie

3 egg whites
½ teaspoon baking powder
½ teaspoon salt
1 cup sugar

1 cup graham cracker crumbs
1 teaspoon vanilla
1 cup chopped pecans
Whipped cream

Beat egg whites, baking powder, and salt until stiff. Gently add sugar, graham cracker crumbs, vanilla, and pecans. Bake at 350º in a greased 8-inch square pan for 25 minutes. Let cool and loosen around edges. Top with whipped cream.

Carole T. Ray, Greenwood Council and Ethel Comeaux,
Gulf Coast Council (Book 1)

Chocolate Chip Blonde Brownies

⅔ cup butter, melted
2 cups brown sugar
2 eggs
2 cups all-purpose flour
¼ teaspoon baking soda

1 teaspoon salt
2 teaspoons vanilla extract
1 (6-ounce) package chocolate
  chip morsels

Combine first 3 ingredients, then add flour, baking soda, and salt. Mix well and add vanilla. Spread in greased 9x9x2-inch pan. Sprinkle with chocolate chips. Bake at 350º for 20–25 minutes. Cool and cut into squares. Makes 2 dozen brownies.

Betty Blake, Pioneer, Greenwood Council (Book 2)

Chocolate Caramel Brownies

1 (14-ounce) package Kraft
   caramels, unwrapped
⅔ cup evaporated milk,
   divided

1 (18¼-ounce) box German
   chocolate cake mix
¾ cup margarine, softened
1 cup chopped pecans

Melt caramels with ⅓ cup evaporated milk; set aside. Combine cake mix, remaining ⅓ cup evaporated milk, and margarine. Stir in nuts. Put half of cake mixture in greased 9x13-inch pan. Spread batter with greased hands. Bake at 350º for 6 minutes. Top with caramel mixture. Spread remaining cake mixture on top. Return to oven for 15–18 minutes. Cool before cutting.

Anna Earls (Book 3)

Chocolate Chip Bars

2 eggs
1½ cups brown sugar
¾ cup cooking oil
1 teaspoon vanilla extract
1½ cups all-purpose flour

1½ teaspoons baking powder
1 teaspoon salt
½ cup chopped nuts
1 cup chocolate, lemon, or
   butterscotch chips

Mix eggs, brown sugar, oil, and vanilla. Sift together flour, baking powder, and salt. Add to first mixture. Add nuts and chips; mix well. Pour into a greased 9x13-inch pan. Bake 25 minutes at 350º. Cut into bars. Makes 16 servings.

Dorothy Holloway, Jackson, MS (Book 4)

Chewy Pecan Squares

8 eggs, slightly beaten
7 cups brown sugar
3¾ cups biscuit mix
3½ cups chopped pecans

2 tablespoons whipping cream
  or condensed milk
2 teaspoons vanilla extract
Confectioners' sugar

Preheat oven to 350º. Mix eggs and brown sugar in double boiler. Steam for 15 minutes, stirring constantly. Remove from heat and add biscuit mix, chopped pecans, cream, and vanilla. Spread in well-greased 17x25-inch pan and bake 20–25 minutes. Cut while warm and roll in confectioners' sugar.

Martha Minyard, Tupelo Council (Book 2)

Pecan Tassies

SHELLS:

1 (3-ounce) package cream
  cheese, softened

1 stick butter, softened
1 cup all-purpose flour

Cream together cream cheese and margarine until soft. Stir in flour and chill. Shape into 20 (1-inch) balls. Place in ungreased small muffin tins and shape to fit tins.

FILLING:

1 egg
1 tablespoon margarine,
  softened

¾ cup brown sugar
1 teaspoon vanilla extract
1 cup chopped nuts

Mix egg, margarine, brown sugar, and vanilla; add nuts. Place equal amounts Filling into uncooked Shells. Bake at 325º for 20–25 minutes. You may top each one with a whole pecan or a cherry before baking, if desired. Makes 24 (½-inch) tassies.

Rosa Roberts, Greenwood Council (Book 1)

No-Bake Cookies

1 stick margarine
½ cup cocoa
2 cups sugar
½ cup milk

3 cups quick oats
½ cup peanut butter
1 teaspoon vanilla extract

In a saucepan, melt margarine over medium heat. Mix in cocoa, sugar, and milk. Heat until bubbles form around side. Remove from heat and add peanut butter, vanilla, and oats. Drop on wax paper; cool.

Kitty Cuevas, Gulf Coast Council (Book 1)

Forever Amber

4 cups orange slice candy,
  cut up in small pieces
2 (3½-ounce) cans Angel
  Flake coconut
2 (14-ounce) cans sweetened
  condensed milk

2 cups or more chopped pecans
1 teaspoon vanilla flavoring
1 teaspoon orange flavoring
1 (16-ounce) box confectioners'
  sugar

Mix together all ingredients, except confectioners' sugar, and place in a greased sheet cake pan. Bake for 30 minutes at 275º. Remove from oven and stir in sugar; mix well. Drop by teaspoonfuls on wax paper and let cool completely.

Dorothy S. Thomas, Laurel Club (Book 1)

Peanut Crunch

2 pounds white almond bark
1 cup peanut butter
2 cups dry roasted peanuts

3 cups Rice Krispies
2 cups mini marshmallows

Melt almond bark in large microwave bowl. Stir and add peanut butter; mix well. Add remianing ingredients and mix well. Drop by spoonfuls on wax paper. Allow about 1 hour to dry well and store in airtight container. Makes about 80.

Fredonia L. Granholm, Grenada, MS (Book 4)

Cow Pies

1 tablespoon shortening
2 cups milk chocolate chips
1 teaspoon vanilla extract

½ cup raisins
½ cup chopped almonds

Melt shortening and chocolate chips in double boiler. Remove from heat; pour in vanilla, raisins, and almonds. Drop on wax paper. Put in refrigerator to cool.

Marie Hardy, Grenada, MS (Book 4)

Butterscotch Clusters

2 (6-ounce) packages
  butterscotch chips
1 (8½-ounce) package
  Planter's peanuts

1 (3-ounce) can La Choy
  chow mein noodles

Melt butterscotch chips in a heavy saucepan over low heat, stirring constantly. Remove from heat and quickly stir in nuts and dry noodles until evenly coated. Dip out by spoonfuls onto wax paper or cookie sheet. Chill and refrigerate; store in an airtight container out of refrigerator after they have been chilled.

Inez Knight, Jackson South Council (Book 2)

Peanut Butter Candy

1 cup sugar
1 cup Karo syrup
1 (12-ounce) jar crunchy
  peanut butter

6 cups crushed cornflakes

Combine sugar and Karo syrup in a 6-quart pan. Bring to a boil. Add peanut butter; mix. Stir in cornflakes one cup at a time, and mix. Drop by teaspoonfuls on wax paper. Makes 40–50.

Donna B. Gaddis, Meridian, MS (Book 4)

Peanut Brittle

2 cups sugar
½ cup water
½ cup white Karo corn syrup

2 cups raw peanuts
2 teaspoons baking soda

Mix sugar, water, and syrup; cook on high heat until mixture boils. Add peanuts and continue cooking on ¾ heat until candy is brittle when small amount is dropped in cold water (about 10 minutes). Remove from heat and add soda. Stir fast (will foam). Pour on greased cookie sheet, spreading candy out all over it. When cool and hardened, break into pieces with handle of butter knife.

Angela L. McCoy, Jackson Council (Book 3)

Graham Cracker Pralines

1 (14-ounce) box honey
  graham crackers
1 cup brown sugar
1 cup butter

1 cup nuts, broken into large
  pieces
1 teaspoon vanilla extract

Break single graham crackers down the middle. Cover the bottom of a 13x17½-inch cookie sheet with graham crackers. Be sure cookie sheet has edges turned up on all four sides. Boil sugar, butter, nuts, and vanilla for 2 minutes, being careful not to scorch. Pour over graham crackers; spread with spoon if necessary. Bake in 350º oven for 10 minutes, being careful not to burn. Lift with spatula onto wax paper. If any crackers stick to pan as it cools, just put back in warm oven until they loosen.

Bettie Sue Sullivan (Book 3)

Creamy Pralines

2 cups sugar
1 cup buttermilk
2 tablespoons light Karo syrup
1 teaspoon baking soda

1 stick butter
1 teaspoon vanilla extract
Dash of salt
1½ cups chopped pecans

Combine sugar, buttermilk, Karo syrup, baking soda, and butter in a 4-quart heavy saucepan. Cook to soft-ball stage (238º), stirring frequently; remove from heat. Add vanilla and salt; beat well until mixture begins to thicken. Add pecans and drop from teaspoon onto wax paper.

Note: Takes about 35 minutes on stove; if cooked too long it will be grainy; if undercooked it won't be firm. The soft ball in cold water test works also.

Vistan Allen, Collinsville, MS (Book 4)

Twice-Cooked Divinity

2 cups sugar
½ cup Karo syrup
½ cup water
Dash of salt

2 egg whites, beaten until stiff
1 teaspoon vanilla extract
1 cup pecans

Stir together sugar, Karo syrup, water, and salt. Boil to medium ball stage (240º), stirring constantly. (Heat on 3–4, or medium.) After bringing to a boil (about 8 minutes), pour ⅓ mixture over stiff egg whites in a large bowl, beating constantly. Cook remaining syrup about 8 minutes longer (hard-ball stage); check for string. Beat this syrup into egg white mixture. When mix holds shape when dropped from spoon, add vanilla and pecans; beat 3–5 minutes or until not shiny. Drop onto greased cookie sheet. Do not cover; leave open to dry out.

Eleanor Johnson, Jackson South Council; Malindia (Sissy) Finley, Greenwood Life Member Club; Lynn Ainsworth, Jackson South Council; Mrs. Everetta Kimbreil, Meridian Council (Book 1)

Buttermilk Caramel Fudge

2 cups sugar
3 tablespoons white Karo
 syrup
1 cup buttermilk

1 teaspoon baking soda
1 cup chopped pecans
1 tablespoon butter or margarine
1 teaspoon vanilla extract

Mix sugar, Karo syrup, buttermilk, and baking soda in boiler. Stir well; cook until it forms a medium hard ball when dropped in cold water. Add pecans, butter, and vanilla; beat until cool and creamy. Pour in well-greased platter. When cooled, cut in squares.

Note: Adding baking soda to the sugar, Karo syrup, and buttermilk is what turns this to caramel.

Rosa Roberts, Greenwood Council (Book 1)

Old-Fashioned Chocolate Fudge

To make good fudge, it requires beating the mixture for a long time. My mother gave me this recipe. She makes the creamiest, most delicious candy I have ever eaten.

2 cups sugar
3 tablespoons Hershey's cocoa
¾ cup milk
⅓ cup white Karo syrup

4 tablespoons butter
1 teaspoon vanilla extract
1 cup chopped pecans (optional)

Combine sugar and cocoa in a heavy 2-quart saucepan and mix thoroughly. Add milk and Karo syrup and stir over medium heat until dissolved. Continue to cook mixture slowly without stirring until a small portion dropped in cold water forms a very soft ball. Do not overcook. Remove from heat; add butter and vanilla. Allow mixture to cool 2–3 minutes; beat until mixture begins to harden. Add pecans and pour into buttered dish.

Charles J. LeBlanc, Jackson North Council (Book 1)

Millionaire's Fudge

4½ cups sugar
1 (12-ounce) can evaporated
  milk
1 stick butter
2 cups marshmallow crème
1 (12-ounce) package chocolate
  chips

8 (1.55-ounce) plain Hershey's
  bars, chopped
2 cups (or more) coarsely
  chopped pecans

Bring sugar, evaporated milk, and butter to a boil. Boil 3 minutes, stirring constantly. Remove from stove and add marshmallow crème, chocolate chips, and Hershey's bars. Stir until melted and blended. Stir in pecans. Working quickly, drop with two teaspoons onto wax paper. Makes a lot of pieces.

Betty and Gene Cryder, Madison, MS (Book 4)

Buckeyes

2 sticks margarine, softened
2 cups smooth peanut butter
1½ (16-ounce) boxes
  confectioners' sugar

1 (12-ounce) package chocolate
  chips
Paraffin (almost 1 stick)

Mix and work together margarine, peanut butter, and sugar until smooth. Roll into balls and refrigerate overnight.

Melt chocolate chips and paraffin in a double boiler. Put a toothpick into the balls and dip into chocolate mixture, leaving top uncovered, to resemble buckeyes.

Ouva Green, Meridian Council (Book 1)

Rum Balls

1 cup crushed vanilla wafers
1 cup confectioners' sugar
1 cup chopped pecans
2 tablespoons cocoa
2 tablespoons white Karo syrup

¼ cup rum
½ cup sugar
Extra chopped pecans for
   rolling candy

Combine crushed vanilla wafers, confectioners' sugar, 1 cup pecans, and cocoa. Add Karo syrup and rum; mix well. Shape into 1-inch balls; roll half of balls in granulated sugar and remaining in pecans.

Doris P. Kelly, Jackson North Council (Book 2)

Orange Coconut Balls

1 (12-ounce) box vanilla wafers
1 stick butter or margarine,
   softened
1 (6-ounce) can frozen orange
   juice

1 (16-ounce) box confectioners'
   sugar
½–¾ cup chopped nuts
Coconut as needed

Crush vanilla wafers; add all other ingredients except coconut. Form into balls and roll in coconut. I put mine in refrigerator for a while after making them. These also freeze well.

Sadie Patterson, Meridian Council (Book 2)

Martha Washington Candy

1 stick butter, softened
1 (14-ounce) can sweetened
  condensed milk
2 (16-ounce) boxes
  confectioners' sugar
1 teaspoon vanilla extract

3 cups chopped pecans
1 cup flaked coconut (optional)
1 (16-ounce) package milk
  chocolate chips
¾ block paraffin wax

In heavy-duty mixer, place softened butter and condensed milk; beat well. Add a cup of confectioners' sugar at a time, beating well after each addition. Add vanilla, nuts, and coconut, if desired. Put this mixture in airtight container and place in refrigerator. This will be a very stiff, hard mixture.

Put chocolate chips and wax in top of double boiler over hot water. Water should not be boiling but kept right at the boiling point to melt the chips and wax. When chocolate chips and paraffin are liquid, scoop the candy mixture out by teaspoonfuls; form into balls by hand. I make about 36 balls of candy at a time and then stick a toothpick into each ball. Have the top of the double boiler tilted and still sitting over the hot water. Holding the candy ball by the toothpick, dip it into the melted chocolate and rake off the candy ball with another toothpick onto wax paper.

Note: This recipe will make hundreds of balls but can be kept in refrigerator until ready for another batch. The chocolate chips will solidify and can be reheated whenever needed.

Vistan Allen, Collinsville, MS (Book 4)

Candy Strawberries

2 (3-ounce) packages
  strawberry Jell-O
1 cup ground pecans
1 cup flaked coconut
¾ cup condensed milk
½ teaspoon vanilla extract

1 (5-ounce) package sliced
  almonds
Green food coloring
Red decorating sugar
Green decorating sugar

Combine dry Jell-O mix, pecans, and coconut; stir in condensed milk and vanilla. Mix well. Chill for at least 1 hour.

Place almonds in bowl; stir in green food coloring, just enough to tint. Spread on paper towels to dry.

Shape chilled Jell-O mixture into strawberry shapes. Roll the slender end of candy in the red sugar. Dip the fat end in the green sugar; insert a sliver of almond in the top for the stem.

Myrtle Hancock, Jackson South Council (Book 1)

Caramel Popcorn

1 stick butter
¼ cup light corn syrup
1 cup light brown sugar

½ teaspoon salt
½ teaspoon baking soda
3 quarts popcorn, popped

In a glass bowl, combine first 4 ingredients and cook in microwave on HIGH for 2 minutes. Remove and stir. Cook for 2 more minutes. Remove and stir. Add baking soda and stir until foamy. Place popped popcorn in large paper bag, not recycled. Pour mixture over popcorn. Shake bag well and place in microwave. Cook on HIGH for 1½ minutes. Remove and shake well. Microwave for 1½ minutes more. Remove and shake well. Microwave for 45 seconds. Remove and shake again. Microwave for 30 seconds. Remove and shake, then place on cookie sheet and cool. Store in airtight container. Use less popcorn if you prefer more caramel on the popcorn.

Blanche Maxwell (Book 3)

Pies and Other Desserts

1980
Cordless

Cordless phones first appeared around 1980 and were primitive by today's standards. These phones, without cables or cords, chiefly used radio frequency and were initially given a frequency of 27 MHz by the Federal Communications Commission (FCC), which is the same frequency range used by CB radio. The base needs a separate power source to transmit the signal to the handset. The cordless handset is powered by a battery that is recharged by the base station. By 1998 Caller ID was introduced, 2.4 GHz frequencies opened, and a Digital Spread Spectrum signal became available. This added security and spread the signal 360 degrees from the base to the handset, so there were no dead spots and distance could go to a quarter mile. As additional features were added, prices dropped and demand rose. Consumers now wanted all their phones to be cordless. This created a new set of problems. If there was ever a power failure, you wouldn't have any working phones.

Easy Pie Crust

2½ cups flour
1½ teaspoons salt

⅔ cup oil
⅓ cup ice water

Sift and measure flour; sift together with salt. Measure and pour oil and water into quart jar with tight lid. Shake thoroughly until thick and creamy white. Pour over flour mixture and stir with fork just enough to form dough ball. Halve dough and roll between wax paper. Makes 2 pie crusts. If you need to bake the crust prior to adding filling, bake at 375º for 10–12 minutes or until golden brown.

Annie O. Edwards, Clarksdale Club (Book 2)

Fresh Blueberry Pie

5 cups blueberries, rinsed
  and dried gently
2 teaspoons lemon juice
1 cup sugar
3 tablespoons cornstarch

Pinch of cinnamon
1 tablespoon cold butter,
  cut into bits
Pastry for double crust pie
  (see Easy Pie Crust recipe)

Toss berries with lemon juice in a large bowl. In a separate bowl, mix sugar, cornstarch, and cinnamon; toss this mixture with berries and transfer to pastry-lined pie plate. Dot with butter and fit the top crust; seal and flute. Brush pastry with a little milk or cream and sprinkle with additional sugar. Cut several vents in the top crust. Bake in preheated 375º until the pie is golden brown and filling is bubbly, about 40 minutes. Serve warm with vanilla ice cream.

Dot Trinkner, Jackson North Council (Book 3)

Blackberry Pie

1½ cups blackberries
1½ cups sugar, divided
1 pie shell, unbaked

½ cup self-rising flour
⅔ stick margarine
¾ cup milk

Wash berries; sprinkle with ½ cup sugar. Pour into pie shell. Mix flour and remaining 1 cup sugar. Pour over berries. Put margarine slices on top. Pour milk over top of margarine. Bake at 350º for 1 hour.

Jessie M. (Mrs. Joe T.) Crawford, Lena, MS (Book 4)

Crumbly Apple Pie

7 apples, thinly sliced
½ cup granulated sugar
1 teaspoon ground cinnamon

¼ teaspoon ground nutmeg
¼ teaspoon salt
1 (9-inch) deep-dish pie crust

Mix apple slices, sugar, cinnamon, nutmeg, and salt; pour into pie shell.

TOPPING:

¾ cup firmly packed dark
    brown sugar
¾ cup all-purpose flour

½ teaspoon nutmeg
⅓ cup butter, chilled, cut into
    small pieces

Mix Topping ingredients together and cut in butter until coarse crumbs form. Sprinkle evenly over apples. Cook in preheated 400º oven on lowest rack for 35 minutes or until lightly browned. If pie is over-browning; cover loosely with aluminum foil.

Juanita Shipp, Jackson, MS (Book 4)

Fresh Strawberry Pie

1 quart fresh strawberries,
  sliced
1 pie crust, precooked
¾ cup sugar
3 tablespoons cornstarch
10 ounces 7-Up, Fresca, or
  Sprite

½ teaspoon salt
½ (3-ounce) package
  strawberry Jell-O
Cool Whip or whipped cream,
  for topping

Place sliced berries in cooked pie crust. Cook sugar, cornstarch, 7-Up, and salt until mixture thickens; add Jell-O and cool. Pour over berries and chill until firm. Top with Cool Whip or whipped cream.

Louise B. Hardy, Greenwood Council (Book 1)

Strawberry Pie

1 pint frozen strawberries,
  thawed, drained
1 (14-ounce) can condensed
  milk
1 cup chopped pecans

⅓ cup lemon juice
1 (8-ounce) container frozen
  Cool Whip, thawed
2 graham cracker pie crusts

Combine strawberries, milk, pecans, and lemon juice. Add Cool Whip last and put in crust. Chill. Top with additional whipped cream if desired.

Joan and Dave Robertson, Jackson, MS (Book 4)

Strawberry Pie

No sugar!

2 tablespoons cornstarch
1½ cups boiling water
1 (3-ounce) box sugar-free
  strawberry Jell-O
4 individual packages Equal,
  or to taste

1 pint or more fresh
  strawberries, sliced
1 graham cracker crust
Cool Whip, for topping

Dissolve cornstarch in a little cold water; add to boiling water and Jell-O. Boil for about 2 minutes or until thick. Let cool. Add Equal and pour in strawberries. Pour into graham cracker crust; chill. Top with Cool Whip.

Chris Watts, Greenwood Council (Book 3)

Caramel Pie

1¼ cups brown sugar
1 cup milk
1 stick margarine
Pinch of salt

4 tablespoons flour
1 egg, beaten
1 teaspoon vanilla
1 (9-inch) pie shell, baked

Combine brown sugar, milk, margarine, salt, flour, and egg in double boiler and cook until thick; add vanilla. Pour into baked pie shell. Let set, then serve.

Frankie Miller, Greenwood Life Member Club (Book 2)

Caramel Pecan Pie

36 Kraft caramels, unwrapped
¼ cup water
¼ cup butter
¾ cup sugar
¼ teaspoon salt

½ teaspoon vanilla
3 eggs
1 cup pecan halves
1 (9-inch) unbaked pie shell

Melt caramels with water and butter in covered double boiler or in a saucepan over low heat. Combine sugar, salt, vanilla, and eggs. Gradually add caramel sauce and mix well. Stir in pecan halves. Pour into pastry shell. Bake at 350° for 45 minutes. Pie filling will appear to be very soft, but becomes firmer as it cools.

Vesta B. Walker, Gulf Coast Council, Biloxi Gulf Sands Life Member Club (Book 1)

Pecan Pie

1 cup sugar
¼ cup margarine, melted
½ cup white Karo syrup
3 eggs, slightly beaten

1 cup chopped pecans
1 teaspoon vanilla
Dash of salt
1 (9-inch) pie crust, unbaked

Preheat oven to 350º. Mix sugar, margarine, and Karo syrup. Add eggs. Add pecans, vanilla, and salt. Pour in unbaked pie crust. Bake at 350º for 15 minutes; turn oven down to 300º and continue to bake for 25 minutes.

Sherry Till, Jackson North Council (Book 1)

Fudge Pecan Pie

So happy to share my recipe.

1 (9-inch) pastry shell, unbaked
½ cup sugar
⅓ cup Hershey's cocoa
⅓ cup all-purpose flour, unsifted
¼ teaspoon salt

3 eggs
3 tablespoons butter, melted
1½ teaspoons vanilla
½ cup chopped pecans
½ cup pecan halves
Whipped cream (optional)

Prepare pastry shell (or use already prepared pastry shell); set aside. Combine remaining ingredients, except pecans, in mixer bowl; beat on medium speed for 30 seconds (do not overbeat). Stir in chopped pecans; pour into shell. Arrange pecan halves on top. Bake at 350° for 1 hour; cool. For full flavor, cover and let stand for 1 day before serving. Serve with whipped cream, if desired.

Sheila Moore, Jackson Council (Book 3)

Chocolate Chip Pie

1 cup sugar
½ cup flour
2 eggs, well beaten
1 stick margarine, melted
1 teaspoon vanilla

1 cup semisweet chocolate bits
¾ cup chopped pecans
½ cup flaked coconut
1 deep-dish pie shell, unbaked

Blend sugar, flour, eggs, margarine, and vanilla well. Stir in chocolate bits, pecans, and coconut. Pour into pie shell and bake at 350° for 30–35 minutes, or until firm.

Mary Jane Horn, Cleveland Club, Boyle, MS (Book 4)

My Mother's Old-Fashioned Chocolate Pie

4 eggs, divided	2 cups milk, divided
¾ cup sugar	2 tablespoons butter
4 tablespoons flour	1 teaspoon vanilla flavoring
4 tablespoons cocoa	

Separate 3 egg whites and set aside for Meringue. In a large bowl, beat egg yolks and the additional egg together. In another bowl, mix sugar, flour, and cocoa together until there are no lumps. Add 1 cup milk to egg yolk mixture; mix well. Add cocoa mixture to milk-egg mixture. Pour into double boiler. Add remaining cup milk, butter, and vanilla flavoring. Cook until butter is melted. Pour into heated pie crust and bake at 375º until firm. While pie is baking, make Meringue.

MERINGUE:

1 cup sugar, divided	Cream of tartar (optional)
3 egg whites (from above)	

Add ½ cup sugar to egg whites and beat well. When this stands in a peak, add remaining ½ cup sugar and beat until all sugar is dissolved and Meringue is in a stiff peak. Use a dash of cream of tartar, if desired. Top baked pie with Meringue and then place pie back in oven until Meringue is golden brown.

Darothy B. Doster, Tupelo Council (Book 3)

Chocolate Chess Pie

1½ cups sugar
1 (5-ounce) can evaporated
   milk
½ cup butter, melted
3 tablespoons cocoa
1 teaspoon vanilla
2 eggs

½ cup chopped pecans
1 (9-inch) pie shell
Cool Whip for garnish
   (optional)
Chocolate shavings for garnish
   (optional)

Put first 6 ingredients in blender; mix well. Add pecans. Pour in pie shell and bake at 350º for 30–35 minutes. Let cool. Top with Cool Whip and chocolate shavings, if desired.

Theresa Buchanan (Book 3)

Old-Fashioned Chess Pie

2 cups sugar
2 heaping tablespoons flour
1 heaping tablespoon cornmeal
1 stick butter, melted

3 eggs, beaten
½ cup buttermilk
2 teaspoons vanilla
1 (12-inch) pie shell, unbaked

Combine sugar, flour, and cornmeal; mix well. Add butter and mix well. Add beaten eggs, mixing well. Add buttermilk and vanilla; blend thoroughly. Pour mixture into pie shell and bake at 425º for 10 minutes. Reduce temperature to 325º and bake 30 more minutes. When pie begins to brown, cover with a sheet of aluminum foil to prevent deep browning or burning.

Eleanor Wells (Pioneer Partner), Greenwood Council (Book 1)

Lemon Chess Pie

1 stick butter, softened
1½ cups sugar
3 eggs
2 tablespoons flour

Juice of 2 lemons
1 tablespoon grated lemon rind
1 (9-inch) pie shell, unbaked

Cream butter and sugar; add eggs, flour, lemon juice, and grated lemon rind. Pour into unbaked pie shell. Bake 1 hour at 250º. Serve with whipped cream.

Brenita Deflanders, Gulf Coast Council (Book 2)

Buttermilk Pie

ONE PIE:
1½ cups sugar
1 stick butter, softened
3 eggs
2 tablespoons flour

½ cup buttermilk
1 teaspoon vanilla
¼ teaspoon coconut extract
1 pie shell, unbaked

TWO PIES:
2¼ cups sugar
1½ sticks butter, softened
4 eggs
3 tablespoons flour

¾ cup buttermilk
1½ teaspoons vanilla
½ teaspoon coconut extract
2 pie shells, unbaked

THREE PIES:
3 cups sugar
1½ sticks butter, softened
6 eggs
4 tablespoons flour

1 cup buttermilk
2 teaspoons vanilla extract
1 teaspoon coconut extract
3 pie shells, unbaked

Preheat oven to 400º. Cream sugar and butter; add eggs and flour alternately. Add buttermilk, vanilla, and coconut extract. Pour in pie shell(s). Set oven at 350º. Cook about 1 hour or until filling doesn't shake.

Dot Trinkner, Jackson North Council (Book 1)

French Coconut Pie

3 eggs
1 cup sugar
½ cup margarine, melted

½ cup white corn syrup
1 (9-inch) pie shell, unbaked
¾ cup flaked coconut

Beat eggs, sugar, margarine, and corn syrup well. Pour into unbaked pie shell. Sprinkle coconut on top. Bake at 350º for about 45 minutes or until golden brown.

Virginia Clark, Jackson South Council (Book 2)

Coconut Pie

This makes its own crust.

4 eggs, beaten well
½ cup self-rising flour
1¾ cups sugar

1 teaspoon vanilla
½ stick margarine, melted
1 (7-ounce) can flaked coconut

Combine all ingredients. Mix well and pour into 2 (9-inch) pie pans. Bake at 325º for 30 minutes, or until brown. Makes 2 (9-inch) pies.

Mildred Thompson, Meridian Council (Book 3)

Never Fail Coconut Pie

1 stick margarine or butter,
  softened
1½ cups sugar
3 eggs, well beaten
1 teaspoon vanilla

1 tablespoon vinegar or
  lemon juice
1 cup fresh or frozen flaked
  coconut
1 (9-inch) pie shell, unbaked

Combine all ingredients and pour into unbaked pie shell. Bake for 1 hour at 350º.

Doris P. Kelly, Jackson North Council (Book 1)

Sweet Potato Pie

2 cups cooked, mashed sweet
  potatoes
1 cup firmly packed brown
  sugar
½ cup butter or margarine,
  softened
2 eggs, separated
½ teaspoon ground ginger
½ teaspoon ground cinnamon
½ teaspoon ground nutmeg
¼ teaspoon salt
½ cup evaporated milk
¼ cup sugar
1 (9-inch) deep-dish pastry shell
Whipped topping (optional)

Combine sweet potatoes, brown sugar, butter, egg yolks, spices, and salt in a large mixing bowl; beat until light and fluffy. Add evaporated milk; mix just until combined. Beat egg whites until foamy; gradually add sugar, beating until stiff. Fold stiffly beaten egg whites into potato mixture; pour into pie shell. Bake at 400° for 10 minutes; reduce heat to 350° and bake an additional 45–50 minutes or until set. Cool and top with whipped topping, if desired.

J. W. Wilkinson, McComb Club (Book 1)

Sweet Potato Pie

Charley Pride's mother's recipe.

1 (9-inch) pie shell, unbaked
1 cup mashed sweet potatoes,
  hot
½ cup butter, melted
2 eggs, beaten
⅓ cup half-and-half or milk
½ teaspoon baking powder
½ teaspoon nutmeg
1 teaspoon vanilla extract

Prepare pie shell (or buy prepared crust from supermarket and set aside). Combine sweet potatoes with remaining ingredients, blending well by hand with a wooden spoon. Pour into pie shell. Bake in preheated 400° oven for about 30 minutes, or until golden brown and puffy. Serve alone or topped with sweetened cream.

Lynette Thomas (Book 3)

George Washington Pie

1⅓ cups plain flour
1 cup chopped pecans
1 stick margarine, softened
2 (8-ounce) packages cream
  cheese, softened

1 cup confectioners' sugar
2 (32-ounce) cans cherry pie
  filling
2 cups Cool Whip

Mix flour, pecans, and margarine together. Pack into a 9x13-inch glass dish. Bake for 20 minutes in a 400º oven. Let cool. Mix cream cheese and sugar; cream well. Spread on cooled crust. Layer cherry filling on top of cream cheese. Spread Cool Whip over cherry filling and let chill.

Blanche B. Millsap, Jackson Council (Book 3)

Berry Cobbler

¼ cup butter, softened
1 cup sugar, divided
1 egg
1 cup flour
2 teaspoons baking powder

¼ teaspoon salt
½ cup milk
1½ cups blackberries or
  raspberries
1 cup berry juice

Cream together until light and fluffy the butter, ½ cup sugar, and egg. Sift together the flour, baking powder, and salt. Mix alternately with the milk, the dry mixture, and the sugar-egg mixture. Beat until smooth. Pour batter into greased 11½x7½x1⅛-inch pan or 10-inch casserole.

Sprinkle remaining ½ cup sugar over berries. Spoon over batter and pour berry juice over top. Bake 45 minutes in 375º oven. During baking, fruit and juice will go to bottom and a cake-like layer forms on top. Serve with cream. Serves 6.

Annie O. Edwards, Pioneer Clarksdale Club (Book 1)

Ambrosia

1 ripe banana, peeled and
  sliced diagonally
1 (13½-ounce) can pineapple
  chunks, drained, reserve juice

3 medium oranges, sectioned
1 cup seedless grapes, halved
⅔ cup flaked coconut
½ cup ginger ale (optional)

Dip bananas into reserved pineapple syrup. Arrange half of each fruit in a bowl; top with half the coconut, then layer rest of fruit. Pour pineapple syrup over; chill. At serving time, pour ginger ale over top, if desired. Top with remaining coconut. Makes 4–6 servings.

Bubbles Talbot, Gulf Coast Council (Book 1)

Strawberry Trifle

Delicious!

1 (5-ounce) box vanilla instant
  pudding mix
3–4 cups milk
1 prepared angel food cake

1½ pints fresh strawberries
1 (8-ounce) tub frozen Cool
  Whip, thawed

Prepare pudding mix according to package directions with milk. Crumble angel food cake into medium-size pieces. Place some of the pieces in a large bowl (a clear glass bowl is prettier). Pour a layer of vanilla pudding on top of cake pieces. Arrange with a layer of sliced strawberries and a layer of Cool Whip. Repeat layers with Cool Whip at top of bowl. Garnish top with 3–4 whole strawberries.

Bonnie Nowell, Jackson North Council (Book 1)

Strawberry Delight

1 (20-ounce) can crushed
pineapple, drained, reserve
juice
1 (3-ounce) box strawberry
Jell-O

24 large marshmallows
1 (2.6-ounce) package
Dream Whip
2 cups cottage cheese

Combine pineapple juice, dry Jell-O, and marshmallows in saucepan. Melt over low heat, stirring constantly until well dissolved; let cool slightly. While cooling, whip Dream Whip according to package instructions. Add cooked mixture to pineapple and cottage cheese, then fold in Dream Whip; refrigerate. Takes approximately 3 hours to set firmly. Serves about 6.

Variation: Add ½ cup chopped pecans.

Yvonne Roberson, Natchez Council (Book 2)

Quick Apple Dumplings

2 (21-ounce) cans apple pie
filling
⅔ cup water
1 teaspoon butter or margarine

1 (10-count) canned
refrigerator biscuits
Cinnamon-sugar mixture to taste

Mix apple filling with water. Put in a large skillet with tight-fitting lid. Add butter; bring to a boil over medium heat. Cut each biscuit in 4 pieces. Sprinkle biscuit pieces with cinnamon-sugar mixture. Drop biscuit pieces into bubbling apples. Reduce heat to simmer on low. Cover and cook for 30 minutes; do not lift lid until biscuits are cooked. Serve at once with milk or cream.

Sheila Moore (Book 3)

Apple Crisp

6 apples, peeled and sliced
½ cup firmly packed light
  brown sugar
1 tablespoon cinnamon
1½ cups graham cracker crumbs
3 tablespoons butter, melted

Put layer of apples in a dish. Mix sugar and cinnamon together, and sprinkle some on apples. Continue to layer until all is used. Top with graham cracker crumbs and melted butter. Bake at 350º for 30 minutes.

Bessie Henley, Gulf Coast Council (Book 1)

Country Apple Dessert

1 (18¼-ounce) box yellow
  cake mix
½ cup butter
2 eggs, divided
1 (21-ounce) can apple pie
  filling
½ cup brown sugar
¼ cup chopped walnuts
  (optional)
1 cup sour cream
1 teaspoon vanilla

Mix cake mix, butter, and 1 egg; pat into bottom of 9x13-inch pan. Cover with apple pie filling. Mix brown sugar and walnuts; sprinkle over apple filling. Mix sour cream, remaining egg, and vanilla; drizzle over pie filling. Bake at 350º for approximately 40–50 minutes.

Linda Swearingen, Tupelo Council (Book 3)

Apple Pie Pizza

1 (18¼-ounce) package cake
  mix
1¼ cups quick-cooking rolled
  oats, divided
2 ounces (½ cup) shredded
  Cheddar cheese
8 tablespoons margarine or
  butter, softened, divided

1 egg
½ cup firmly packed brown
  sugar
¼ cups chopped nuts
1 (21-ounce) can apple pie
  filling

Heat oven to 350º. Grease 12-inch deep-dish pizza pan or 9x13-inch pan. In large bowl, combine dry cake mix, 1 cup oats, cheese, and 6 tablespoons margarine at low speed until crumbly. Reserve 1 cup crumbs for topping. To remaining crumbs, blend in egg. Press in prepared pan. Bake at 350º for 12 minutes.

To reserved crumbs, in same large bowl, add remaining ¼ cup oats, 2 tablespoons margarine, brown sugar, and nuts. Mix thoroughly. Spread pie filling over cooked crust. Sprinkle evenly with reserved crumb mixture. Return to oven and bake for 15–20 minutes or until crumbs are light golden brown. Cool completely. Cut into wedges or squares. If desired, serve with whipped cream or ice cream. Serves 12.

Martha Alice Minyard, Tupelo Council (Book 3)

Old-Fashioned Egg Custard

1 cup milk
2 egg yolks
2 tablespoons sugar

½ teaspoon salt
¼ teaspoon vanilla

Scald milk in double boiler. Beat egg yolks, sugar, and salt. Pour milk slowly over egg mixture, then return to double boiler and cook, stirring constantly, about 5 minutes or until custard coats spoon. Cool and add vanilla. Serve warm or cold.

Pat Denham, Jackson South Council

Custard Flan

1 cup sugar
2 egg yolks
3 whole eggs
1 (14-ounce) can condensed
  milk

14 ounces sweet milk
1 (3-ounce) package cream
  cheese, softened
1 teaspoon vanilla

Caramelize sugar by melting over low heat into a clear golden to dark brown syrup. This will reach a temperature from 320°–356°. Pour caramelized sugar into a 9-inch glass baking dish. Place all other ingredients in blender and blend at high speed for 7 minutes. Pour over caramelized sugar. Place dish in a pan partially filled with water and bake for 1 hour at 350°. Let cool and refrigerate for 8 hours or more before serving. Decorate with fruit such as strawberries or kiwi, if desired.

Lois Lewis, Clinton, MS (Book 2)

Katherine's Banana Pudding

1 (5-ounce) package vanilla
  instant pudding mix
1 (14-ounce) can Eagle Brand
  sweetened condensed milk
1 (8-ounce) carton frozen Cool
  Whip, thawed
1 (12-ounce) box vanilla wafers
6–8 bananas, sliced

Mix vanilla pudding as directed on box; add sweetened condensed milk. Fold in Cool Whip. Layer wafers, bananas, and pudding, ending with pudding. Makes 1 extra large bowl or 2 medium bowls of pudding.

Katherine Scott, Natchez Council (Book 2)

Banana Pudding

1 (12-ounce) box vanilla wafers
6 bananas, sliced
1 cup sugar, divided
2 tablespoons flour
¼ teaspoon salt
2 cups milk
3 eggs, separated
1 teaspoon vanilla

Arrange a layer of ½ the vanilla wafers in a 9x13-inch baking dish. Layer with ½ the sliced bananas; set aside. Thoroughly mix ¾ cup sugar, flour, and salt. Add milk, egg yolks, and vanilla; cook until thick; do not boil. Put half on top of bananas in baking dish, and repeat layers with remaining wafers, bananas, and pudding. Beat egg whites until stiff. Add remaining ¼ cup sugar and beat. Put this meringue on top and brown in 350º oven for about 15 minutes or until meringue is slightly golden.

Mildred Lauderdale, Clarksdale Club (Book 2)

Bread Pudding

3 eggs, beaten
1½ cups sugar
1 teaspoon vanilla
½ cup margarine, softened
1 (14-ounce) can sweetened
  condensed milk

⅔ cup hot water
8 slices bread
1 tablespoon cinnamon (or just
  enough to sprinkle over top)
½ cup chopped pecans (more
  or less to sprinkle over top)

Combine eggs, sugar, vanilla, margarine, and condensed milk; beat well. Add hot water and beat again with mixer. Pour over bread that has been broken into small pieces, in a greased 10x13-inch pan. Top with cinnamon and chopped pecans. Bake at 375º until brown; allow to set (about 15 minutes). Serve with Sauce.

SAUCE:

1 stick margarine
¾ cup sugar
1 tablespoon flour

½ cup milk
½ teaspoon vanilla

Mix all and cook until slightly thick.

Variation: Substitute 1 teaspoon rum flavoring for vanilla.

Betty Staples, Laurel, MS (Book 4)

Bread Pudding

1 loaf French bread
4 cups milk, divided
3 eggs
2 cups sugar

2 tablespoons vanilla
1 cup raisins
3 tablespoons margarine, melted

Cut up bread and soak in 1 cup milk; crush with hands until well mixed. Add eggs to remaining 3 cups milk and beat well. Add sugar, vanilla, and raisins and stir well. Combine with the bread mixture. Pour melted margarine into bottom of baking pan, then pour pudding mixture into pan and bake at 350º for 30–35 minutes. Serve warm with Whiskey Sauce.

WHISKEY SAUCE:

1 stick butter, softened
1 cup sugar

1 egg, well beaten
Whiskey

Cream together butter and sugar, then cook in double boiler until very hot and well dissolved. Add well-beaten egg and whip really fast so egg doesn't curdle. Let cool and add whiskey to taste.

Sherry Till, Jackson North Council

In 1978, American Telephone and Telegraph's (AT&T) Bell Laboratories began testing a mobile telephone system based on hexagonal geographical regions called cells. As the caller's vehicle passed from one cell to another, an automatic switching system would transfer the telephone call to another cell without interruption. The cellular telephone system began nationwide usage in the United States in 1983.

Primo's Donut Pudding

9 donuts
½ cup sugar

3 cups milk
1 tablespoon lemon flavoring

Dice donuts and place in 2½-inch deep baking pan; sprinkle with sugar. Pour in milk and lemon flavoring; stir. Bake at 350° until golden brown.

CUSTARD SAUCE:
2½ cups milk
2½ cups sugar
3 tablespoons flour

Margarine, melted
1 tablespoon lemon flavoring

Heat milk; mix sugar with flour and enough melted margarine to dissolve sugar, and add to milk. Add lemon flavoring. Pour Custard Sauce over pudding and serve.

Chet Wells, Jackson North Council (Book 1)

Cookies and Cream

1 (16-ounce) package Oreo
  cookies, crushed
1 (8-ounce) package cream
  cheese, softened
1 stick butter, softened
1 cup powdered sugar

1 (8-ounce) tub frozen Cool
  Whip, thawed
2 (3-ounce) packages vanilla
  instant pudding
3 cups milk
1 teaspoon vanilla

Put half the crushed cookies in 9x13-inch pan. Mix cream cheese and margarine. Mix in powdered sugar. Fold in Cool Whip. In a separate bowl, mix together pudding mix, milk, and vanilla. Fold cream cheese mixture into pudding mixture. Pour over cookie crumbs. Sprinkle remainder of cookie crumbs on top. Refrigerate to set. This also can be frozen.

Mary Clemons (Book 3)

Chocolate Sin

CRUST:

1½ cups self-rising flour   ¾ stick margarine, melted
1 cup chopped pecans

Mix together and press into a 9x13-inch baking dish. Bake at 350º
for 20 minutes; let cool.

LAYER 1:

1 (8-ounce) package cream   1 cup powdered sugar
  cheese, softened   1 cup Cool Whip

Mix all 3 ingredients and beat until smooth. Spread over crust.

LAYER 2:

1 (5-ounce) or 2 (3-ounce)   1 teaspoon vanilla
  packages chocolate instant   Cool Whip, to cover
  pudding

Prepare pudding mix according to instructions on package; add
vanilla. Spread over cream cheese layer. Top with Cool Whip.
Can wait until just before serving to add Cool Whip on top.
Refrigerate.

Beth Harbour, Meridian Council (Book 2)

Easy Chocolate Ice Cream

1 (14-ounce) can sweetened
condensed milk

1 (16-ounce) can chocolate syrup
½ gallon milk

Mix all 3 ingredients together and freeze in electric ice cream freezer until it slows down or stops.

Marylyn Lee, Jackson Council (Book 3)

Delicious Homemade Ice Cream

Tastes liked cooked custard without all the work.

2 (14-ounce) cans sweetened
condensed milk
2 (12-ounce) cans evaporated
milk

1 (3-ounce) package vanilla
instant pudding
2 teaspoons vanilla
½ gallon whole sweet milk

Combine condensed milk and evaporated milk. Mix pudding according to directions on box. Add vanilla. Add mixtures and sweet milk up to fill line of ice cream freezer. Makes 1 gallon.

Peggie Brown, Jackson North Council (Book 2)

Chocolate Almond Ice Cream

½ gallon chocolate milk
2 (14-ounce) cans sweetened
  condensed milk

1 (5½-ounce) can toasted almond
  slivers

Mix together and freeze in 1-gallon ice cream freezer. Will start to slow down and stop when ready.

Marylyn Lee, Jackson Council (Book 3)

Butter Pecan Ice Cream

1½ cups chopped pecans
3 tablespoons butter, melted
3 (5-ounce) cans evaporated
  milk
2½ cups sugar

1 teaspoon butter flavoring
1 (5-ounce) box vanilla instant
  pudding mix
Milk, enough to fill container

Coat pecans in melted butter and toast in glass dish in microwave until you can smell them, 4–5 minutes; taste them, they may need a few more minutes. Mix butter, evaporated milk, sugar, flavoring, and pudding together; may use mixer. Add with toasted pecans and enough whole milk to fill up ice cream freezer.

Note: I use 1 box of ice cream salt in making this.

Betty Staples, Laurel, MS (Book 4)

Snow Ice Cream

1½–2 cups heavy cream or
   whipping cream, chilled
2 tablespoons vanilla extract,
   chilled

1 large bowl (ice cold) fresh,
   clean snow
1¼ cups powdered sugar

Mix cream and vanilla and pour over freshly fallen snow in bowl; add powdered sugar until well blended. Be careful not to let it melt. Add more snow if ice cream is too thin or more sugar if not sweet enough. Eat immediately! Make flavor variations by substituting chocolate or other extracts for the vanilla.

Frances Barnes, Tupelo Life Member Club (Book 4)

Orange Sherbert

1 (2-liter) bottle Orange Crush
2 (15-ounce) cans sweetened
   condensed milk

1 (16-ounce) can crushed
   pineapple, undrained

Combine ingredients and freeze in a 1-gallon ice cream freezer.

Frances Breeden, Jackson, MS (Book 4)

Amaretto Freeze

½ gallon vanilla ice cream
⅔ cup amaretto

½ cup triple sec
½ cup crème de cacao

Combine all ingredients in blender. Pour into freezer-safe dish and freeze for several hours or overnight. Serve in individual dessert dishes.

Dora T. Tidwell, Tupelo Council (Book 2)

Sour Cream Dessert Cupsy

2 cups thick sour cream
¾ cup sugar
2 tablespoons lemon juice
Dash of salt
1 (7-ounce) can crushed
  pineapple, drained

½ cup chopped nuts
3 tablespoons maraschino
  cherries, drained and finely
  chopped

Line muffin pans with paper cups. Mix sour cream, sugar, lemon juice, and salt. Blend in pineapple, nuts, and cherries. Spoon mixture into baking cups and freeze, about 3 hours. Makes 12 cups.

Margaret Nail, Tupelo Council (Book 1)

Cream Cheese Tarts

2 (8-ounce) packages cream
  cheese, softened
1 cup sugar
2 eggs

1 teaspoon vanilla
12 vanilla wafers
Blueberry, cherry, or favorite
  pie filling

Beat cream cheese and sugar together until light and fluffy; add eggs and vanilla. Place a vanilla wafer in each paper-lined muffin tin. Spoon cream cheese mixture over wafer, filling cups full. Bake at 350º for 20 minutes. Chill overnight. Top with small amount of pie filling to serve. Yields 12 servings.

Helen Funk, Ruth, MS (Book 4)

Yam and Apple Delight

TOPPING:

¾ cup instant rolled oats
4 tablespoons all-purpose flour
¾ cup dark brown sugar

⅓ cup butter or margarine,
softened

Mix together rolled oats, flour, and brown sugar. Cut in butter until evenly mixed and crumbly. Set aside.

APPLE SAUCE MIXTURE:

1 (16-ounce) jar applesauce,
chunky style, divided
1 teaspoon cinnamon, divided

1 (16-ounce) can yams, cut to
bite size

Arrange a little less than ½ the applesauce in a 6x10x2-inch baking dish. Sprinkle with ½ teaspoon cinnamon. Spoon 3 tablespoons of prepared Topping over the applesauce base. Evenly arrange yams. Add remaining applesauce to cover yams. Sprinkle with remaining ½ teaspoon cinnamon. Add the remaining topping and spread evenly. Bake at 350º until heated throughout, 30–40 minutes. Serve plain, hot, or for a special added touch, top with whipped cream or 2 scoops of vanilla ice cream.

Elaine Gaddis (Book 3)

Banana Split Cake

FIRST LAYER:

2 cups crushed graham
    crackers

6 tablespoons butter, melted
6 tablespoons powdered sugar

Combine to make crust. Spread in bottom of square casserole dish.

SECOND LAYER:

2 cups powdered sugar
2 egg whites

1 stick margarine, softened

Combine and mix for 10 minutes; pour over First Layer.

THIRD LAYER:

3–5 bananas

Slice the bananas lengthwise and place over Second Layer.

FOURTH LAYER:

1 (20-ounce) can crushed pineapple, well drained

Spread drained pineapple over Third Layer.

FIFTH LAYER:

1 (8-ounce) tub frozen Cool Whip, thawed

Spread Cool Whip over Fourth Layer.

SIXTH LAYER:

1 cup chopped pecans
1 cup chopped cherries

1 (24-ounce) bottle Hershey's
    chocolate syrup

Spread pecans and cherries over Fifth Layer. Chill. Just before serving, drizzle chocolate syrup over cake.

Gail Lang, Meridian Council (Book 1)

Banana Fritters

¾ cup all-purpose flour
1 teaspoon baking powder
⅛ teaspoon salt
¼ cup granulated sugar
1 egg, beaten

⅓ cup milk
2 tablespoons melted
  shortening
Shortening for frying
6 bananas

Sift together first 3 ingredients; add sugar. Combine egg, milk, and shortening; add to dry ingredients. Stir only enough to mix well. Heat additional shortening slowly to 375º in a deep kettle. Halve bananas lengthwise and once across. Dip each piece into batter. Fry in hot shortening for 5–6 minutes until golden brown. Drain, then place on absorbent paper. Serve hot with Lemon Sauce (below).

Brenda Beck, Tupelo Council (Book 1)

Lemon Sauce

1¼ tablespoons flour
⅔ cup sugar
⅛ teaspoon salt

1¼ cups boiling water
1½ tablespoons oil
1½ tablespoons lemon juice

Combine sugar, flour, and salt, and mix thoroughly. Gradually pour into boiling water. Add oil, stirring constantly. Bring to boiling point and boil 5 minutes. Add lemon juice and serve hot.

Mary Alice Hydrick, Jackson North Council (Book 1)

Equivalents, Substitutions, Etc.

EQUIVALENTS:

Apple: 1 medium = 1 cup chopped

Banana: 1 medium = 1/3 cup

Berries: 1 pint = 1¾ cups

Bread: 1 slice = ½ cup soft crumbs = ¼ cup fine, dry crumbs

Broth, beef or chicken: 1 cup = 1 bouillon cube dissolved in 1 cup boiling water

Butter: 1 stick = ¼ pound = ½ cup

Cabbage: 2 pounds = 9 cups shredded or 5 cups cooked

Cheese, grated: 1 pound = 4 cups; 8 ounces = 2 cups

Chicken: 1 large boned breast = 2 cups cooked meat

Chocolate, bitter: 1 square or 1 ounce = 2 tablespoons grated

Coconut: 3½-ounce can = 1⅓ cups

Cool Whip: 8 ounces = 3 cups

Cornmeal: 1 pound = 3 cups

Crabmeat, fresh: 1 pound = 3 cups

Crackers, graham: 15 = 1 cup crushed

Crackers, saltine: 23 = 1 cup crushed

Cream, heavy: 1 cup = 2–2½ cups whipped

Cream cheese: 3 ounces = 6⅔ tablespoons

Egg whites: 8–10 = 1 cup

Eggs: 4–5 = 1 cup

Evaporated milk: 5⅓-ounce can = ⅔ cup; 12-ounce can = 1¼ cups

Flour: 1 pound = 4½ cups

Flour, self-rising: 1 cup = 1 cup all-purpose + 1½ teaspoons baking powder + ½ teaspoon salt

Garlic powder: ⅛ teaspoon = 1 average clove

Gingerroot: 1 teaspoon = ¾ teaspoon ground

Grits: 1 cup = 4 cups cooked

Herbs, fresh: 1 tablespoon = 1 teaspoon dried

Lemon: 1 medium = 3 tablespoons juice

Marshmallows: ¼ pound = 16 large; ½ cup = 4 large

Milk, whole: 1 cup = ½ cup evaporated + ½ cup water

Mushrooms: ¼ pound fresh = 1 cup sliced

Mustard, dry: 1 teaspoon = 1 tablespoon prepared

Noodles: 1 pound = 7 cups cooked

Nuts, chopped: ¼ pound = 1 cup

Onion: 1 medium = ¾–1 cup chopped = 2 tablespoons dried chopped (flakes)

Orange: 3–4 medium = 1 cup juice

Pecans: 1 pound shelled = 4 cups

Potatoes: 1 pound = 3 medium

Rice: 1 cup = 3 cups cooked

Spaghetti: 1 pound uncooked = 5 cups cooked

Spinach, fresh: 2 cups chopped = 1 (10-ounce) package frozen chopped

Sugar, brown: 1 pound = 2½ cups

Sugar, powdered: 1 pound = 3½ cups

Sugar, white: 1 pound = 2¼ cups

Vanilla wafers: 22 = 1 cup fine crumbs

Equivalents, Substitutions, Etc.

SUBSTITUTIONS:

1 slice cooked bacon = 1 tablespoon bacon bits

1 cup buttermilk = 1 cup plain yogurt; or 1 tablespoon lemon juice or vinegar + plain milk to make 1 cup

1 cup sifted cake flour = 7/8 cup sifted all-purpose flour

1 ounce unsweetened chocolate = 3 tablespoons cocoa + 1 tablespoon butter or margarine

1 ounce semisweet chocolate = 3 tablespoons cocoa + 1 tablespoon butter or margarine + 3 tablespoons sugar

1 tablespoon cornstarch = 2 tablespoons flour (for thickening)

1 cup heavy cream (for cooking, not whipping) = 1/3 cup butter + 3/4 cup milk

1 cup sour cream = 1/3 cup milk + 1/3 cup butter; or 1 cup plain yogurt

1 cup tartar sauce = 6 tablespoons mayonnaise or salad dressing + 2 tablespoons pickle relish

1 cup tomato juice = 1/2 cup tomato sauce + 1/2 cup water

1 cup vegetable oil = 1/2 pound (2 sticks) butter

1 cup whipping cream, whipped = 6–8 ounces Cool Whip

1 cup whole milk = 1/2 cup evaporated milk + 1/2 cup water

MEASUREMENTS:

3 teaspoons = 1 tablespoon

1 tablespoon = 1/2 fluid ounce

2 tablespoons = 1/8 cup

3 tablespoons = 1 jigger

4 tablespoons = 1/4 cup

8 tablespoons = 1/2 cup or 4 ounces

12 tablespoons = 3/4 cup

16 tablespoons = 1 cup or 8 ounces

3/8 cup = 1/4 cup + 2 tablespoons

5/8 cup = 1/2 cup + 2 tablespoons

7/8 cup = 3/4 cup + 2 tablespoons

1/2 cup = 4 fluid ounces

1 cup = 1/2 pint or 8 fluid ounces

2 cups = 1 pint or 16 fluid ounces

1 pint, liquid = 2 cups or 16 fluid ounces

1 quart, liquid = 2 pints or 4 cups

1 gallon, liquid = 4 quarts or 8 pints or 16 cups

OVEN-TO-CROCKPOT CONVERSIONS:

15–30 minutes in the oven = 1½–2½ hours on HIGH or 4–6 hours on LOW

35–45 minutes in the oven = 2–3 hours on HIGH or 6–8 hours on LOW

50 minutes–3 hours in the oven = 4–5 hours on HIGH or 8–10 hours on LOW

Index

1983
Cellular

The development of commercial cellular systems did not occur rapidly—almost 36 years passed between the initial concept in 1947 and the debut of the first commercial systems in 1983. Much of this delay was due to regulatory discussions. However, the delay ultimately allowed developers to incorporate many new supporting technologies such as microprocessors and integrated circuits, which were developed during this interim period, into the design of the cellular telephone as we know it. The term "cellular" began as a term for analog service transferred from cell to cell, but is now used as a general term for all wireless phone services. By 1987, cellular telephone subscribers exceeded one million and the airways were crowded. The industry began to research new transmission technology, and by 1991, system capacity increased 1000% with both analog and digital capability, and new data features such as fax and messaging services were in the works. Today, there are more than 60 million wireless customers, and advances in mobile telephony continue to drive the industry.

Index

Index

Index

Index

Index

Index

Index

These cookbooks make perfect gifts for any occasion.

Bell's Best	Bell's Best 2	Bell's Best 3 Savory Classics	Bell's Best 4 The Next Generation	Best of the Best from Bell's Best Cookbook
788 pages	690 pages	756 pages	498 pages	288 pages
6 x 9 • Index	6 x 9 • Index	6 x 9 • Index	6 x 9 • Index	6 x 9 • Index
Paper bound	Paper bound	Paper bound	Paper bound	Comb bound
$12.00	$12.00	$12.00	$12.00	$18.95

Prices include postage and handling.

You can also order our cookbooks online from our Pioneer e-store at **www.bellsouthmspioneers.org**.

- -

Bell's Best Order Form

Make check payable to **Telephone Pioneers** and send with Order Form to:
Mississippi Chapter No. 36 • BellSouth Pioneers
P. O. Box 811 • Jackson, MS 39205

Name _____

Address _____

City/State/Zip _____

Phone # _____

Email Address _____

QUANTITY	TITLE *(Postage and handling included)*	EACH	COST
	Bell's Best	$12.00	
	Bell's Best 2	$12.00	
	Bell's Best 3: Savory Classics	$12.00	
	Bell's Best 4: The Next Generation	$12.00	
	Best of the Best from Bell's Best	$18.95	
Note: U.S. currency only.		**TOTAL**	

BEST OF THE BEST STATE COOKBOOK SERIES

Best of the Best from
ALABAMA
288 pages, $16.95

Best of the Best from
ALASKA
288 pages, $16.95

Best of the Best from
ARIZONA
288 pages, $16.95

Best of the Best from
ARKANSAS
288 pages, $16.95

Best of the Best from
BIG SKY
Montana and Wyoming
288 pages, $16.95

Best of the Best from
CALIFORNIA
384 pages, $16.95

Best of the Best from
COLORADO
288 pages, $16.95

Best of the Best from
FLORIDA
288 pages, $16.95

Best of the Best from
GEORGIA
288 pages, $16.95

Best of the Best from the
GREAT PLAINS
North and South Dakota, Nebraska, and Kansas
288 pages, $16.95

Best of the Best from
HAWAI'I
288 pages, $16.95

Best of the Best from
IDAHO
288 pages, $16.95

Best of the Best from
ILLINOIS
288 pages, $16.95

Best of the Best from
INDIANA
288 pages, $16.95

Best of the Best from
IOWA
288 pages, $16.95

Best of the Best from
KENTUCKY
288 pages, $16.95

Best of the Best from
LOUISIANA
288 pages, $16.95

Best of the Best from
LOUISIANA II
288 pages, $16.95

Best of the Best from
MICHIGAN
288 pages, $16.95

Best of the Best from the
MID-ATLANTIC
Maryland, Delaware, New Jersey, and Washington, D.C.
288 pages, $16.95

Best of the Best from
MINNESOTA
288 pages, $16.95

Best of the Best from
MISSISSIPPI
288 pages, $16.95

Best of the Best from
MISSOURI
304 pages, $16.95

Best of the Best from
NEVADA
288 pages, $16.95

Best of the Best from
NEW ENGLAND
Rhode Island, Connecticut, Massachusetts, Vermont, New Hampshire, and Maine
368 pages, $16.95

Best of the Best from
NEW MEXICO
288 pages, $16.95

Best of the Best from
NEW YORK
288 pages, $16.95

Best of the Best from
NO. CAROLINA
288 pages, $16.95

Best of the Best from
OHIO
352 pages, $16.95

Best of the Best from
OKLAHOMA
288 pages, $16.95

Best of the Best from
OREGON
288 pages, $16.95

Best of the Best from
PENNSYLVANIA
320 pages, $16.95

Best of the Best from
SO. CAROLINA
288 pages, $16.95

Best of the Best from
TENNESSEE
288 pages, $16.95

Best of the Best from
TEXAS
352 pages, $16.95

Best of the Best from
TEXAS II
352 pages, $16.95

Best of the Best from
UTAH
288 pages, $16.95

Best of the Best from
VIRGINIA
320 pages, $16.95

Best of the Best from
WASHINGTON
288 pages, $16.95

Best of the Best from
WEST VIRGINIA
288 pages, $16.95

Best of the Best from
WISCONSIN
288 pages, $16.95

All cookbooks: 6x9 inches, ringbound, contain photographs, illustrations and index.

To order by credit card, call toll-free **1-800-343-1583**
or visit our website at **www.quailridge.com.**

☒ Order form

Use this form for sending check or money order to:
QUAIL RIDGE PRESS • P. O. Box 123 • Brandon, MS 39043

❏ Check enclosed

Charge to: ❏ Visa ❏ MC ❏ AmEx ❏ Disc

Card # _____

Expiration Date _____

Signature _____

Name _____

Address _____

City/State/Zip _____

Phone # _____

Email Address _____

Qty.	Title of Book (State) or Set	Total

Subtotal	_____
7% Tax for MS residents	_____
Postage ($4.00 any number of books)	+ 4.00
Total	_____